EGYPTIAN BOOK OF THE DEAD

THE EGYPTIAN HIEROGLYPHIC
TEXT EDITED FROM NUMEROUS PAPYRUS

BY

WALLIS E. A. BUDGE

Copyright © 2018 Read Books Ltd.
This book is copyright and may not be
reproduced or copied in any way without
the express permission of the publisher in writing

British Library Cataloguing-in-Publication Data
A catalogue record for this book is available from
the British Library

A RETURN TO EGYPT

There is a land where Time no count can keep,
  Where works of men imperishable seem;
  Where through death's barren solitude doth gleam
Undying hope for them that sow and reap :
Yea, land of life where death is but a deep
  Warm slumber, a communicable dream,
  Where from the silent grave far voices stream
Of those who tell their secrets in their sleep.

Land of the palm-tree and the pyramid,
  Land of sweet waters from a mystic urn,
    Land of sure rest where suns shine on for ever,
I left thee—in thy sands a heart was hid,
    My life, my love, were cast upon thy river,
  And, lo ! to seek Osiris I return.

H. D. Rawnsley,
Notes for the Nile, 1892

THE PRINCIPAL GEOGRAPHICAL AND MYTHOLOGICAL PLACES IN THE BOOK OF THE DEAD

Ȧbṭu 🕊️ 𓂋 𓈖 𓅯 𓌉, the Abydos of the Greeks and the ⲉⲃⲱⲧ of the Copts, was the capital of the eighth nome of Upper Egypt. It was the seat of the worship of Osiris in Upper Egypt, and the god was believed to have been buried there. For many centuries its priests boasted the possession of the head of Osiris, and the great annual miracle-play, in which the sufferings, death, and resurrection of Osiris were acted, drew thousands of people to the festival from every part of Egypt. Local tradition made the sun to end its daily course at Abydos, and to enter into the Ṭuat at this place through a " gap " in the mountains called in Egyptian *peq*,

𓊪 𓂝 𓇳. These mountains lay near to the town; and in the XIIth dynasty it was believed that the souls of the dead made their way into the Other World by the valley which led through them to the Great Oasis, where some placed the Elysian Fields.[2] Under the New Empire the tomb of King Khent at Abydos was identified by local tradition as the tomb of Osiris, and it became the object of pilgrimages from every part of Egypt. Under the XXIInd dynasty the cult of Osiris declined, and the town never regained the importance which it had enjoyed under the XVIIIth dynasty.

Ȧmenta or **Ȧmentet,** 𓋀 𓏏, or 𓋀 𓏏 𓈇, was originally the place where the sun set, but subsequently the name was applied to all the cemeteries which were built in the stony plateaus and mountains on the western bank of the Nile. Some believe that Ȧmenta was, at first, the name of a small district, without either funereal or mythological signification. The Christian Egyptians, or Copts, used the word Ȧmenti to translate the Greek word Hades, to which they attributed all the ideas which their heathen ancestors had associated with the Āmenta of the Book of the Dead.

Ānu, the Heliopolis of the Greeks (Herodotus, II, 3, 7, 8, 9, 59, 93; Strabo, XVII, i, 27 ff.), was the capital of the thirteenth nome of Lower Egypt. The Hebrews called it On (Genesis xli, 45, 50; xlvi, 20), Aven (Ezekiel xxx, 17), and Bêth-Shemesh (Jeremiah xliii, 13); this last name is an exact translation of the Egyptian *per Rā*, "house of the sun," which was also a designation of Ānu. The Copts have preserved the oldest name of the city under the form ⲱⲛ. A Coptic bishop of this place was present at the Council of Ephesus. The city of Ānu seems to have become associated with the worship of the sun in prehistoric times. Already in the Vth dynasty its priesthood had succeeded in gaining supremacy for their religious views and beliefs throughout Egypt, and from first to last it maintained its position as the chief seat of the cult of Rā. The body of the Aged One, a name of Osiris, reposed in Ānu, and there dwelt the Eye of Osiris. The deceased made his way to Ānu, where souls were joined unto bodies in thousands, and where the blessed dead lived on celestial food for ever.

Ān-ruṭf, or **Naāruṭf**, was a section of the Ṭuat of Herakleopolis; the meaning of the name is "the place where nothing groweth."

Ān-ṭes (?), an unknown locality where, the tower of a Light-god (?), was adored.

Āpu, the Panopolis of the Greeks (Πανῶν πόλις, Strabo, XVII, i, 41), was the metropolis of the ninth nome of Upper Egypt, and the seat of the worship of the god, whose name is variously read Āmsi, Khem, and Menu. In ancient days it was famous as the centre for stone cutting and linen weaving, and the latter industry still survives among the modern Coptic population, who, following their ancestors, call their city ⲯⲙⲓⲙ, which the Arabs have rendered by Akhmîm.

Ȧkert 𓈎𓇳𓏏, a common name for the abode of the dead.

Bast 𓎯𓏏, more fully Pa-Bast, or Per-Bast 𓉐𓎯𓏏𓆇, the Bubastis of the Greek writers (Herodotus, II, 59, 137, 156, 166; Strabo, XVII, i, 27), the metropolis of the eighteenth nome of Lower Egypt, and the seat of the worship of Bast, a goddess who was identified with the soul of Isis, *ba en Ast* 𓅡𓏤𓈖𓊨𓏏. The city is mentioned in the Bible under the form פִּי בֶסֶת (Ezekiel xxx, 17), Pi-beseth, which the Copts have preserved in their name for the city, ⲡⲟⲩⲃⲁⲥⲧⲓ; the Arabs call the place Tell Basṭah تل بسطة.

Ḥet-benbent 𓉗𓃀𓈖𓃀𓈖𓏏, the name given to many sun-shrines in Egypt and the Sûdân, and also to one of the places in the Other World where the deceased dwelt.

Ḥet-Ptaḥ-ka 𓉗𓊪𓏏𓎛𓂓, the sacred name of the city of Memphis, the metropolis of the first nome of Lower Egypt; it means the "House of the *ka* of Ptaḥ," and was probably in use in the period of the Ist dynasty. Other names for Memphis were 𓊅𓏤𓏏𓊖, Āneb-ḥetchet, "the city of the white wall"; Men-nefer 𓏠𓈖𓄤𓏤𓊖; and Khā-nefert 𓈍𓂝𓄤𓏏𓊖.

Kam-ur 𓈎𓅓𓅨𓂋, a name given to the district of the fourth and fifth nomes of Upper Egypt.

Khemenu 𓐍𓏠𓈖𓏌𓏤𓊖, 𓐍𓏠𓈖𓊖, *i.e.*, the city of the eight great cosmic gods, the Hermopolis of the Greek writers (Ἑρμοπολιτικη φυλακή, Strabo, XVII, 1, 41), was the metropolis of the fifteenth nome of Upper Egypt. The old Egyptian name for the city is preserved in its Coptic and Arabic names, ϣⲙⲟⲩⲛ and Eshmûnên.

Kher-āḥa 𓐍𓂋𓂝𓊖, a very ancient city which was situated on the right bank of the Nile, a little to the south of Ȧnu, near the site of which the "Babylon of Egypt" (ⲃⲁⲃⲩⲗⲱⲛ ⲛ̄ⲧⲉ ⲭⲏⲙⲓ, the Βαβυλών, φρούριον ἐρυμνόν of Strabo, XVII, i, 30) was built.

Manu 𓃀𓈗 or 𓈗𓈗, is the name given to the region where the sun sets, which was believed to be exactly opposite to the district of Bekha, 𓊪𓈗, where he rose in the east; Manu is a synonym of west, just as Bekha is a synonym of east.[1]

Nekhen 𓊏, or 𓈗𓈗, the name of the shrine of the goddess Nekhebet, which is supposed to have been near to Nekheb, the capital of the third nome of Upper Egypt and the Eileithyiaspolis of the Greeks.

Neter-khertet, or **Khert Neter,** 𓊹𓇯𓈗 or 𓊹𓈗, a common name for the abode of the dead; it means the "divine subterranean place."

Pe 𓊪, a district of the town of Per-Uatchet, 𓉐𓊪𓈗𓊖, the Buto of the Greeks (Βοῦτος, Strabo, XVII, i, 18), which was situated in the Delta.

Per-Àsàr 𓉐𓊨𓊖, "House of Osiris," the Busiris of the Greek writers. It was situated in the Delta, and was the centre of the cult of Osiris in Lower Egypt.

Punt 𓊪𓈖𓏏𓈉, the tropical district which lay to the south and east of Egypt, and which included, in later times, a part of the Arabian peninsula and the eastern coast of Africa along and south of Somaliland.

Ra-stau 𓂋𓊃𓈗 or 𓂋𓊃𓊖, a name given to the passages in the tomb which lead from this to the Other World; originally it designated the cemetery of Ṣakḳârah only, and its god was Seker, later Seker-Àsàr.

Sa 𓅭𓅭𓊖, the Saïs of the Greeks (Σάϊς, Strabo, XVII, i, 23), the metropolis of the fifth nome of Lower Egypt, and the seat of the worship of the goddess Neith.

---

[1] See Brugsch, *Dict. Géog.*, pp. 199, 260; Maspero, *Études de Mythologie*, t. I, p. 332; and *Aeg. Zeitschrift*, 1864, pp. 73–76.

Sekhem, or , the Letopolis of the Greeks, and capital of the Letopolites nome (Strabo, XVII, i, 30); it was the seat of the worship of Ḥeru-ur , "Horus the elder," and one of the most important religious centres in Egypt.

Sekhet-Aanru , *i.e.*, "Field of the Reeds," was a name originally given to the islands in the Delta, or to the Oases, where the souls of the dead were supposed to live. Here was the abode of the god Osiris, who bestowed estates in it upon those who had been his followers, and here the beatified dead led a new existence and regaled themselves upon food of every kind, which was given to them in abundance. According to the vignette of the CXth Chapter of the Book of the Dead, the Sekhet-Áanru is the third division of the Sekhet-ḥetepu, or "Fields of Peace," which have been compared with the Elysian Fields of the Greeks.

Set Amentet , *i.e.*, "the mountain of the Underworld," a common name of the cemetery, which was usually situated in the mountains or desert on the western bank of the Nile.

Suten-ḥenen , more correctly **Ḥensu**, the metropolis of the twentieth nome of Upper Egypt, called by the Greeks Herakleopolis Magna (Strabo, XVII, i, 35). The Hebrews mention the city Hanes (חָנֵס, Isaiah xxx, 4) as the representative of Upper Egypt, and in Coptic times it was still of considerable size and importance; the Copts and Arabs have preserved the ancient name of the city under the forms ⲅⲛⲏⲥ and اهناس, *Ahnas*.

Tanenet , a district sacred to the gods Osiris and Ptaḥ; it was probably situated near Memphis.

Ta-tchesert , *i.e.*, the Holy Land, a common name for the Other World.

Tep ⟨hieroglyph⟩, a district of the town Per-Uatchet ⟨hieroglyph⟩, the Buto of the Greeks (Strabo, XVII, i, 18), which was situated in the Delta.

Teṭu-t ⟨hieroglyph⟩, a name given both to the metropolis [1] of the ninth nome and to the metropolis [2] of the sixteenth nome of Lower Egypt.

Ṭuat ⟨hieroglyph⟩, a common name for the Other World.

- An excert taken from *The Papyrus of Ani - A reproduction in Facsimile, E. A. Wallis Budge*

DESCRIPTION OF THE PAPYRI.

The Chapters of the Book of the Dead, hymns, etc., printed in this and in the following volumes are edited from the following papyri:—

I. THE PAPYRUS OF NEBSENI. This papyrus was acquired by Burton in the early years of the XIXth century, and was sold to the Trustees of the British Museum after his death in the year 1836. As it was impossible to use the papyrus in roll form, first, because of its peculiarly brittle nature, and secondly, because of the damaged state of the document when purchased by the Trustees, it was cut into thirty-three sections, which were carefully pasted on paper and mounted under glass. It measures 77 feet, $7^1/_2$ in. in length, and is 1 foot, $1^1/_2$ in. in breadth; it bears the number 9,900, and is commonly known as the "Burton Papyrus". Unfortunately the exact place where the papyrus was found is unknown, but the texture and colour proclaim its Memphite origin, and we shall probably be correct if we assume that it came from

Ṣaḳḳârah. Nebseni certainly lived at Memphis, for he was a priestly official connected with the famous temple of Ptaḥ, and this being so we should naturally expect that he would be buried at Ṣaḳḳârah. Nebseni, 〈𓏥〉, or 〈𓏥〉, was, according to his papyrus, a scribe 〈𓏥〉, and also a "maker of designs in the temples of the North and the South" 〈𓏥〉.[1] In other words, he drafted the texts which were cut on the walls of the temples, and "set out", or made the copies from which the masons worked when cutting the reliefs on the walls, columns, etc. in the temples. His chief duties were connected with the temple of Ptaḥ of Memphis, as we see from the title 〈𓏥〉, or 〈𓏥〉, "draftsman of the temple of Ptaḥ", and he presided over certain of the "mysteries in the temples" 〈𓏥〉. Another title of Nebseni was 〈𓏥〉, i. e., "child of the Sheṭ chamber", but what his duties were in connection with this office is not known.

Nebseni's father was called Thenna 〈𓏥〉, and he is described as the "draftsman of the designs of the Lord of the Two Lands" 〈𓏥〉;

---

1. Or, 〈𓏥〉.

DESCRIPTION OF THE PAPYRI.   XIII

his mother was called Mut-resthà [hieroglyphs], but of her rank and station in life no details are given. Nebseni's wife was called Senseneb [hieroglyphs].

The following are the Chapters of the Book of Coming Forth by Day contained in the Papyrus of Nebseni:—

I, with Vignette, sheet 1; V, sheet 11; VI, with Vignette, sheet 10; XIII, sheet 12; XVII, lines 81—94, sheet 11, lines 100—106, sheet 12, the complete Chapter, with Vignette, sheets 13—15; XVIII, sheet 15; XX, sheet 11; XXII, with Vignette, sheet 5; XXIII, with Vignette, sheet 5; XXVI, with Vignette, sheets 4 and 5; XXX B, with Vignette, sheet 4; XXXVIII A, with Vignette, sheet 12; XLI, sheet 25; XLIV, sheet 12; XLVI, sheet 5; XLVII, with Vignette, sheet 8; XLVIII, sheet 8; L, two copies, sheets 11 and 12; LVI, two copies, sheets 5 and 11; LXII, with Vignette, sheet 4; LXIV, short version, sheet 23, long version sheet 24; LXV, sheet 22; LXXI, with Vignette, sheet 16; LXXII, with Vignette, sheet 3; LXXVI, sheet 8; LXXVII, with Vignette, sheet 2; LXXXI, with Vignette, sheet 3; LXXXIII, with Vignette, sheet 2; LXXXIV, with Vignette, sheet 2; LXXXV, with Vignette, sheet 2; LXXXVI, with Vignette, sheet 2; LXXXVII, with Vignette, sheet 11; LXXXVIII, with Vignette, sheet 11; LXXXIX, with Vignette, sheet 6; XC, with Vignette, sheet 6; XCVI and XCVII, two copies, sheets 8 and

11; XCIX, with Vignette, sheet 3; C, three copies, sheets 5, 10 and 20; CIII, with Vignette, sheet 8; CIV, with Vignette, sheet 8; CV, with Vignette, sheet 4; CVI, three copies, sheets 16, 19, and 24; CVIII, with Vignette, sheet 7; CIX, with Vignette, sheet 8; CX, with Vignette, sheets 17 and 18; CXII, with Vignette, sheet 7; CXIII, with Vignette, sheet 7; CXIV, with Vignette, sheet 7; CXVII and CXVIII, with Vignette, sheet 11; CXIX, with Vignette, sheet 6; CXXV, with three Vignettes, sheets 29—31; CXXXIII, with Vignette, sheet 22; CXXXIV, with Vignette, sheet 6; CXXXVI A, with Vignette, sheet 26; CXXXVI B, with Vignette, sheet 26; CXXXVII A, sheet 24; CXXXVII B, with Vignette, sheet 6; CXLIV and CXLVI, with Vignettes, sheets 2—4; CXLVIII, with Vignettes, sheets 4 and 5; CXLIX, with Vignettes, sheets 27—29; CL, with Vignette, sheet 29; CLI a, two copies, sheet 21; CLIII A, with Vignette, sheet 12; CLV, with Vignette, sheet 10; CLVI, with Vignette, sheet 10; CLX, with Vignette, sheet 10; CLXVI, sheet 21; CLXVII, with Vignette, sheet 22; CLXXII, sheets 32, 33; CLXXIII, sheet 9; CLXXVII, sheet 18; CLXXVIII, sheet 19; CLXXIX, sheet 26, and CLXXX, two copies, sheet 20, and sheet 21.

A photograph of the Nebseni Papyrus was published by the Trustees of the British Museum (*Photographs of the Papyrus of Nebseni in the British Museum*, London, 1876), with a short preface by Dr. Birch; fifty-two of the seventy-seven Chapters (not reckoning

DESCRIPTION OF THE PAPYRI.   XV

duplicates and triplicates) were published by Prof. Naville in his edition of the Theban Recension of the Book of the Dead (*Das Aegyptische Todtenbuch*, Berlin, 1886), and he gave a description of the Papyrus in his *Einleitung* (pp. 48—54) to that work; a French translation of the Papyrus was published by Massy (*Le papyrus Nebseni, exemplaire hiéroglyphique du livre des morts conservé au British Museum, traduit par A. M.*, Gand, 1885, 8vo), and extracts from it, with translations, have been published by Birch, Naville, Pierret and others. The numbers of the Chapters published in the present work are: VI B, XIII, XVII, XVIII A, XX A, XXXVIII A, XLI, XLVI A, L A, LXII A, LXIV, LXXI, LXXII, XCII, XCVII, CIV, CX A, CXIV, CXXI, CXXV, CXXXVI, CXXXVII A, CXXXVII B, CLX, CLXVI, CLXVII, CLXXII, CLXXIII, CLXXVII, and CLXXVIII.

II. THE PAPYRUS OF NU. This papyrus was found at Ḳûrnah, in Western Thebes, in one of the oldest portions of the necropolis, and was acquired by the Trustees of the British Museum in 1890. The papyrus is darkish brown in colour, and measures 65 feet, $3^1/_2$ inches in length, by $13^1/_2$ inches in width; it is mounted on paper, with a wooden backing, in thirty sheets, and bears the No. 10,477 in the British Museum Collection. It is, I believe, the oldest known codex of the Theban Recension of the Book of the Dead, with painted Vignettes, and it may, with little doubt, be considered a product of the first half of the period of the rule of the kings of the XVIIIth dynasty; it is very little later than the papyrus of Nebseni. The papyrus opens with a coloured scene in which the deceased is represented standing in adoration before Osiris, who is seated on a shrine. Only a few of the Chapters, *i. e.*, those of the Transformations, the Ārits, the Pylons, the Domains (Åats), and one or two others have Vignettes. The titles of the Chapters and the Rubrics are in red, and the text proper is written in black throughout. The whole papyrus is most carefully written, and it is the work of one man, perhaps of Nu himself. It must rank as one of the chief authorities for the text of the Theban Recension, for it is no mere undertaker's stock copy, with blank spaces left for inserting the name of the man or woman for whom it was purchased, but a piece of work which bears in every line of it evidence of the care and knowledge of the copyist. The absence of duplicates and triplicates of several Chapters such as we find in the Papyrus of Nebseni and the Papyrus of Ani is remarkable, and seems to show that the copyist kept a list of the Chapters which he had copied, and guided his work accordingly. In the Papyrus of Nu the only Chapter given in duplicate is No. CXXXII.

The Papyrus resembles that of Nebseni in omitting the Introductory Hymns to Rā and Osiris, and the great Judgment Scene, which are characteristic of the illustrated papyri of the last half of the XVIIIth dy-

DESCRIPTION OF THE PAPYRI.　　　XVII

nasty and subsequent periods, and like most of the
oldest papyri it ends with Chapters CXLIX and CL.
It contains a considerable number of Chapters which
have not hitherto been found in papyri of the Theban
Recension, and also a large number of others which
have only been known from single manuscripts. Of
Chapters XXX, XLIV, CXXXVI, and CLIII it gives
two versions, and the various groups of Chapters relat-
ing to special subjects are singularly complete. Of the
antiquity of the Papyrus many proofs might be adduced,
but it will be sufficient to note that the deceased is fre-
quently described as *neb âmakh* ⟨hieroglyphs⟩, as in the case
of Nebseni, and that the word *maā-kheru* is sometimes
written ⟨hieroglyphs⟩ or ⟨hieroglyphs⟩
(see sheet 20, l. 62; sheet 24, l. 54, and compare Chapter XXIX A published from a papyrus at Parma by
Naville (*Todtenbuch*, I, 40, ll. 1 and 7).

The deceased Nu was, as we learn from sheet 11,
l. 16, "the steward of the overseer of the seal", and
he was the son of Âmen-ḥetep, a man who had held a
similar office, and of the lady Senseneb. ⟨hieroglyphs⟩

⟨hieroglyphs⟩. The name of Âmen-ḥetep is common
enough in the XVIIIth dynasty, but the name of Senseneb is rare, and was mostly used in the first half

b

of the XVIIIth dynasty, and in the period preceding it; see the two instances of the name quoted by Lieblein (*Dict. de Noms*, Livr. III, No. 1558, p. 621, and No. 1963, p. 763). To these may be added that of the wife of Nebseni. The name occurs also on stele No. 502 in the British Museum (XVIIIth dynasty), and on the shrine of Ruka, No. 714, also in the British Museum; in the former case it is the name of a son of Sapár ⸻, and in the latter it is the name of the wife of Ruka.

The Papyrus of Nu contains one hundred and thirty-one Chapters, including two versions each of Chapters XXX, LXIV, CXXXVI, and CLIII, which are as follows:—

Chapter	sheet	Chapter	sheet
I	2	XXII	5
II	13	XXIII	5
III	13	XXIV	5
IV	19	XXV	5
V	21	XXVI	5
VI	21	XXVII	5
VII	22	XXVIII	5
VIII	12	XXIX	12
IX	12	XXX A	5
XI	21	XXX B	21
XII	9	XXXI	5
XVII	2, 3	XXXIV	6
XVIII	4	XXXV	6
XXI	9	XXXVI	8

DESCRIPTION OF THE PAPYRI.

Chapter	sheet	Chapter	sheet
XXXVII	8	LXVIII	7
XXXVIII	12	LXXI	7
XL	8	LXXII	7
XLI	6	LXXIV	6
XLII	6	LXXV	13
XLIII	5	LXXVI	9
XLIV	19	LXXVII	10
XLV	6	LXXVIII	13
XLVI	12	LXXIX	8
XLVII	8	LXXXI A	11
L	19	LXXXII	9
LI	8	LXXXIII	10
LII	11	LXXXIV	10
LIII	11	LXXXV	9
LIV	12	LXXXVI	10
LV	12	LXXXVII	11
LVI	12	LXXXVIII	11
LVII	12	LXXXIX	18
LXI	12	XC	8
LXIII A	12	XCI	6
LXIV, with rubric referring to Ḥesep-ti	13	XCII	7
		XCIII	6
		XCIV	12
LXIV, with rubric referring to Men-kau-Rā	20	XCV	7
		XCVI	19
		XCVII	19
LXV	14	XCVIII	9
LXVII	15	XCIX	21

b*

THE BOOK OF THE DEAD.

Chapter	sheet	Chapter	sheet
C	27	CXXXIII	16
CI	27	CXXXIV	17
CII	28	CXXXVI. 1	16
CIII	8	CXXXVI. 2	28
CIV	8	CXXXVI. 3	28
CV	7	CXXXVII A	26
CVI	8	CXXXVIII	19
CVIII	8	CXLIV	26
CIX	12	CXLV	25
CXII	18	CLXVIII	11
CXIII	18	CXLIX	29
CXV	18	CL	30
CXVI	18	CLI	27
CXVII	9	CLII	13
CXVIII	9	CLIII A	20
CXIX	8	CLIII B	20
CXXII	9	CLIV	18
CXXIII	15	CLV	27
CXXIV	10	CLVI	27
CXXV	22—24	CLXXVI	22
CXXVI	24	CLXXIX	15
CXXX	17	CLXXXVII	19
CXXXI	17	CLXXXVIII	19
CXXXII. 1	11	CLXXXIX	19
CXXXII. 2	12	CXC	16

The order of the Chapters in the Papyrus of Nu is as follows:

DESCRIPTION OF THE PAPYRI.

XVII, XVIII, I, XXII, XXIII, XXV, XXVI, XXVII, XXX A, XLIII, XXIV, XXXI, XXXIII, XXXIV, XXXV, LXXIV, XLV, XCIII, XCI, XLI, XLII, LXVIII, XCII, LXIII A, CV, XCV, LXXII, LXXI, CVI, XL, XC, CVIII, XLVII, CIV, CIII, LI, CXIX, XXXVI, XXXVII, LXXIX, CXVII, CXVIII, XXI, XII, CXXII, XCVIII, LXXVI, LXXXV, LXXXII, LXXVII, LXXXVI, CXXIV, LXXXIII, LXXXIV, LXXXI A, LXXXVII, LXXXVIII, CXXXII, CXLVIII, LII, LIII, LXI, XXVIII, LVI, LVII, LIV, XXXVIII, LV, XXIX, XLVI, CIX, IX, CXXXII, XCIV, LXIII B, VIII, LXIV (short version), II, III, CLII, LXXV, LXXVIII, CXC, CXXXIII, LXV, CXXXIII, LXVII, CLXXIX, CXXIII, CXLI, CXXXVI, CXXXIV, CXXX, CXXXI, LXXXIX, CLIV, CXV, CXVI, CXII, CXIII, CXXXVIII, CLXXXVII, CLXXXIX, XLIV, L, CLXXXVIII, IV, XCVI and XCVII, CLIII A, CLIII B, LXIV (long version), XXX B, XI, V, VI, CXIX, VII, CLXXVII, CXXV, CXXVI, CXLV, CXLIV, CXXXVII A, CI, CLVI, CLV, CLI, C, CII, CXXXVI A, CXXXVI B, CXLIX, CL. The following portion of a Chapter is found on sheet 12, l. 7 (compare Chap. XXVIII)

XXII   THE BOOK OF THE DEAD.

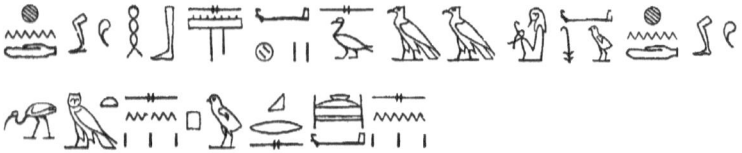

The Chapters printed in the present work are:—
II, III, IV, V, VI, VII, VIII, XI, XXI, XXV, XXVIII,
XXIX, XXX A, XXX B, XXXI, XXXIII, XXXIV,
XXXV, XXXVI, XXXVII, XXXVIII, XL, XLII,
XLIII, XLVI, XLVII, L, LI, LII A, LII B, LIII,
LIV, LV, LVI, LVII, LXIII B, LXIV (two versions),
LXV, LXVII, LXVIII, LXXIV, LXXV, LXXVI,
LXXVII, LXXVIII, LXXIX, LXXXI, LXXXII,
LXXXIII, LXXXIV, LXXXV, LXXXVI, LXXXVII,
LXXXVIII, LXXXIX, XC, XCI, XCIII, XCIV, XCV,
XCVI, XCVII, XCVIII, XCIX, C, CI, CII, CIII,
CIV, CV, CVI, CVIII, CIX, CXII, CXIII, CXV,
CXVI, CXVII, CXVIII, CXIX, CXXII, CXXIII,
CXXIV, CXXV (3 parts), CXXVI, CXXX, CXXXI,
CXXXIII, CXXXIV, CXXXVI A (two versions),
CXXXVI B, CXXXVII, CXXXVIII, CXLI, CXLII,
CXLIV, CXLVI, CXLVIII, CL, CLII, CLIII A
and B, CLIV, CLV, CLVI, CLXXIX, CLXXXVII,
CLXXXVIII, CXC [CXLVIII].

III. THE PAPYRUS OF ANI[1] was found at Thebes,
and was acquired by the Trustees of the British Museum

---

1. See my *Papyrus of Ani in the British Museum*, plates and translation, 2 vols., London, 1895.

in 1888. It is 78 feet long and 15 inches wide, and is the longest known papyrus of the Theban Recension. It is made of six distinct lengths of papyrus which have been joined together with great neatness. The text was written by three scribes at least, but the beautiful Vignettes appear to have been painted by one hand. In some instances the artist has occupied so much space that the scribe has been obliged to crowd the text, and at times he has written it on the border. This proves that the Vignettes were drawn before the text was written. The titles of the Chapters, Rubrics, catchwords, etc., are written in red. The text contains many serious errors, and a large section of Chapter XVII has been entirely omitted. The papyrus was probably produced in the latter years of the XVIIIth dynasty, *i. e.*, about B. C. 1400. Of Ani's parentage we know nothing, but he held several important offices both at Thebes and Abydos, for he was a "veritable royal scribe, scribe and registrary of the "offerings of all the gods, overseer of the granaries of "the Lords of Abydos, and scribe of the offerings of "the Lords of Thebes". The scribe Ani married the lady Thuthu, who was a singer and priestess in the Temple of Āmen-Rā at Thebes. The

Chapters from the Papyrus of Ani printed in the present work are: I, II, V, VIII, IX, X, XV, XVII, XVIII, XXII, XXIII, XXIV, XXVI, XXVII, XXIX A and B, XXX B, XLII (tabular form), XLIII, XLIV, XLV, XLVI, LVIII, LIX, LXI, LXXVIII, LXXX, LXXXI (two versions), LXXXIX, XCI, XCIII, CXXV (Parts 1 and 2), CXXXII, CXLVII, CXLVIII, CLXXVI, and CLXXXVI.

IV. THE PAPYRUS OF IUÀU. This interesting papyrus was discovered by Mr. Theodore M. Davis at Thebes, and published, with a description of its contents, by Prof. E. Naville.[1] It is about 30 feet long, and it contains 40 Chapters of the Theban Recension of the Book of the Dead. The papyrus was written for Iuàu, a father-in-law of Àmen-ḥetep III, king of Egypt about B. C. 1450, to which fact its value is chiefly due. It is one of the very few fine copies of the Theban Recension to which a tolerably exact date can be assigned. The Vignettes are well painted, and the text is good, and it contains an interesting version of Chapter I B, in which the names of the Nine Serpents of Àmenti are given with pictures of them. The Chapters from this papyrus printed in the present work are: I, XIII, XVII, LXIII, LXIV (both versions), LXXXI, LXXXII, CXIX, CIV, CX, CXXV (parts 2 and 3), CXXXVI, CXLI, CXLIV, CXLVI, CLI, CLV, and CLVI.

1. *The Funeral Papyrus of Iouiya*, London, 1908.

DESCRIPTION OF THE PAPYRI. XXV

V. THE PAPYRUS OF HUNEFER[1] was found at Thebes, and was purchased by the Trustees of the British Museum from the late Clot Bey in 1852. It is 18 feet long, and $15^{3}/_{8}$ inches wide, and it is the shortest known illustrated text of the Theban Recension. The material is composed of three layers of good papyrus of a light colour. The inscribed text is perfect, and appears to have been the work of two scribes. The titles of the Chapters, catchwords, etc., are in red. The Papyrus was written in the reign of Seti I, about B. C. 1370, and the text states that Hunefer was the king's steward, and the overseer of his cattle; he was also a royal scribe, and a superintendent of Western Thebes ⸻. Hunefer married the lady Nasha ⸻, who was a priestess and a singer in the Temple of Āmen-Rā at Thebes. The texts from this papyrus printed in the present work are the Introductory Hymns to Rā and Osiris; the latter is commonly called Chapter CLXXXIII.

VI. THE PAPYRUS OF MUT-ḤETEP was probably found at Thebes. It was purchased by the Trustees of the

---

1. For a detailed description of the papyrus with texts and translations, see *Facsimiles of the Papyri of Hunefer, Anhai*, etc., London, folio, 1899.

British Museum from Mr. Murray in 1861. It is 9 feet, $9\,^1/_2$ inches long, and $13\,^1/_8$ inches wide; it is mounted under glass in five sheets, and bears the number 10,010. This papyrus was probably written under the XXth dynasty, about B. C. 1150, and is the work of a careful scribe. The deceased was a priestess and singer in the Temple of Àmen-Rā at Thebes [hieroglyphs]. The Vignettes are coloured, and are of peculiar interest; they are figured in my translation of the Book of the Dead with the Chapters which they illustrate. Chapter CLXXIV is a modified copy of a passage in the text of the Pyramid of Unàs, lines 379 to 399. Its appearance along with Chapters of the Theban Recension goes to prove that portions of the older religious texts were made into Chapters by giving them titles and supplying them with Vignettes. The Chapters given in the papyrus are: XV, CLI, CLXVIII, CLXXIV, CLXXV, and CLXXXII, all of which are printed in the present work.

VII. THE PAPYRUS OF NEKHT, a "chief of the bowmen", and "veritable royal scribe", was found at Thebes, and was acquired by the Trustees of the British Museum in 1888. It is 47 feet, $1\,^1/_8$ inches long, and 14 in. wide, and is mounted under glass in twenty-two sheets; it bears the number 10,471. Nekht probably flourished under the XXth dynasty; his wife's name was Thuàu [hieroglyphs]. His papyrus contains a

DESCRIPTION OF THE PAPYRI. XXVII

large number of Chapters, and is specially interesting for its Vignettes, which are well painted; the only text in it printed in the present work is the fine Hymn to Rā, which is found on sheet 21.

VIII. The papyrus of a person whose name is not given. This papyrus was found at Thebes, and was acquired by the Trustees of the British Museum in 1890. It is $15\frac{1}{2}$ feet long, and $11\frac{3}{4}$ inches wide; it is mounted under glass in seven sheets and bears the number 10,478. The central portion of the papyrus is filled with the picture of a hall having a door at each end. The space between the ceiling and floor is divided into three parts: in the first and third of these is a series of short addresses to personages in four sections of the Other World, and in the second division is a series of vignettes illustrating them. These addresses are printed in the present work as Chapter CLXVIII. The papyrus opens with a vignette in which the deceased is seen standing in adoration at a table of offerings in the presence of Osiris; on a standard, before the god, are the four children of Horus, and behind him is Ḥeru-netch-tef. The "Chapter" which accompanies this Vignette reads:—

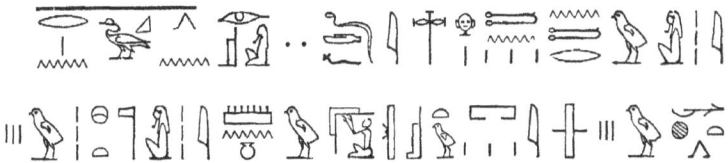

XXVIII   THE BOOK OF THE DEAD.

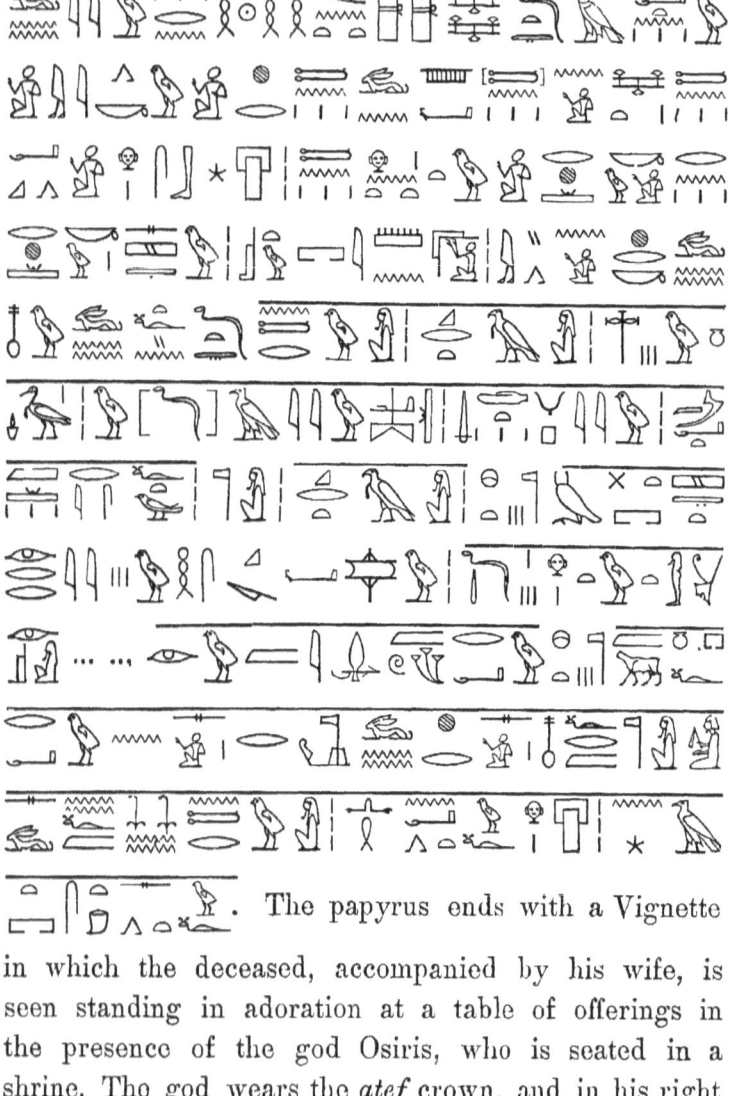 The papyrus ends with a Vignette in which the deceased, accompanied by his wife, is seen standing in adoration at a table of offerings in the presence of the god Osiris, who is seated in a shrine. The god wears the *atef* crown, and in his right hand is the crook, and in the left are the crook and whip,

DESCRIPTION OF THE PAPYRI.   XXIX

emblems of sovereignty and dominion. Behind Osiris stands Isis, who has on her head the disk and horns. The text above the deceased reads: [hieroglyphs]

IX. THE PAPYRUS OF QUEEN NETCHEMET.[1] This papyrus was found at Dêr al-Baḥrî, in Western Thebes, and was purchased by the Trustees of the British Museum in 1894 at the sale of the Egyptian collection of the late General Sir Edward Stanton, K. C. B. It is 13 feet, 3 inches long, and 9 inches wide, and belongs to the period of the XXth dynasty. It bears the number 10,490. It is inscribed in hieratic with versions of Chapters CXLVIII, CXXV (Parts 1 and 2), XIX, CXXIX, CI, CXXXIX and I B, and contains several Vignettes which are also found in some of the later Tombs of the Kings at Thebes. The Chapters from this papyrus printed in the present work are: XIX, CI, CXXXIX and CXLVIII.

X. Several Chapters, Hymns, etc. not found in other papyri are printed from facsimiles and editions of them published by Mariette, Leemans, Lepsius, Naville, Lefébure, Bergmann and others. These are:

1. See my *Facsimiles of the Papyri of Hunefer, Anhai, Ḳerasher, Netchemet*, etc. London, 1899, p. 44.

1. PAPYRUS OF MES-EM-NETER at Cairo, Chapters XIV, XXXIX, LXIX, LXX, CLXIX, and CLXX. See Naville, *Todtenbuch, Einleitung*, p. 74,

2. PAPYRUS OF TURÁ, surnamed NEFER-UBEN-F, Chapters LVII, LXII, CIX, CI and CLXI. See Naville, *Einleitung*, p. 97.

3. PAPYRUS OF NEKHTU-ÁMEN at Berlin, Chapter I B. See Naville, *Einleitung*, 70.

4. PAPYRUS OF ÁMEN-ḤETEP at Cairo, Chapters CXLII, CLXXI. See Mariette, *Les Papyrus Égyptiens*, tome III, Plate 7.

5. PAPYRUS OF QENNA at Leyden, Chapter CLXXXI and two Introductory Hymns. See Leemans, *Papyrus Égyptiens*, tome II, Plate 19.

6. PAPYRUS OF ÁMEN-EM-ḤEB at Paris, Chapter LXVI. See Naville, *Einleitung*, p. 103.

7. PAPYRUS OF PTAḤ-MES (Papyrus Busca), Chapter CXXVII B. See Naville, *Einleitung*, p. 89.

8. PAPYRUS OF SUTIMES at Paris, Chapter CLXXXV. See Guieyesse and Lefébure, *Le Papyrus Funéraire de Soutimes*, Paris, 1877.

9. From a PAPYRUS AT PARIS (No. 3073), Chapter CLXXX; from a PAPYRUS AT PARMA, Chapter XXIX A; from a PAPYRUS AT DUBLIN, Chapter XV B 5. See Naville, *Einleitung*, pp. 86, 96 and 80.

10. From the TOMB OF RAMESES IV, Chapter CXXVII A. See Lefébure, *Tombeau de Ramsés IV*, Paris, 1889, Plate XIII.

11. The TURIN PAPYRUS, edited by Lepsius, Chapters XII, XIX, XX, XXX, XXXII, LX, LXV, LXXIII, CVII, CXX, CXXVIII, CXXIX, CXXXV, CXXXIX, CXL, CXLII, CXLV, CXLVI, CLIV, CLV, CLVI, CLVII, CLVIII, CLIX, CLXII, CLXIII, CLXIV, CLXV.

12. THE COFFIN OF PA-NEḤEM-ȦST at Vienna, Chapters XVIII, and XIX. See Bergmann, *Jahrbuch*, II, 1, 2, Vienna, 1883.

THE CHAPTER OF GIVING A HEART TO OSIRIS

[From the Papyrus of Ani (British Museum No. 10,470, sheet 15).]

THE CHAPTER OF GIVING A HEART TO OSIRIS ANI IN THE UNDERWORLD. He saith:

" May my heart (ab)[1] be with me in the House of Hearts! May my heart (hat) be with me in the House of Hearts! May my heart be with me, and may it rest there, [or] I shall not eat of the cakes of Osiris on the eastern side of the Lake of Flowers, neither shall I have a boat wherein to go down the Nile, nor another wherein to go up, nor shall I be able to sail down the Nile with thee. May my mouth [be given] to me that I may speak therewith, and my two legs to walk therewith, and my two hands and arms to overthrow my foe. May the doors of heaven be opened unto me; may Seb, the Prince[2] of the gods, open wide his two jaws unto me; may he open my two eyes which are blindfolded; may he cause me to stretch apart my two legs which are bound together; and may Anpu (Anubis) make my thighs firm so that I may stand upon them. May the goddess Sekhet make me to rise so that I may ascend unto heaven, and may that be done which I command in the House of the *ka* (double) of Ptah (*i.e.*, Memphis). I understand with my heart. I have gained the mastery over my heart, I have gained the mastery over my two hands, I have gained the mastery over my legs, I have gained the power to do whatsoever my *ka* (double) pleaseth. My soul shall not be fettered to my body at the gates of the underworld; but I shall enter in peace and I shall come forth in peace."

[1] " Ab " is undoubtedly the " heart," and " hat " is the region wherein is the heart; the word may be fairly well rendered by " breast," though the pericardium is probably intended.
[2] " Erpat," i.e., " tribal chief."

- An except from Egyptian Literature, E. A. Wallis Budge, 1901

LIST OF CHAPTERS.

VOLUME I.

I. INTRODUCTORY HYMNS:—

	PAGE
1. Papyrus of Ani	1
2. Papyrus of Qenna	3
3. Papyrus of Qenna	6
4. Papyrus of Hunefer	7
5. Papyrus of Nekht	10
6. Papyrus of Ani	12

LIST OF CHAPTERS. XXXIII

	PAGE
II. Scene of the Weighing of the Heart. Papyrus of Ani	13
1. Names of the gods of the Great Company Papyrus of Ani	13
2. Prayer of the deceased (Chapter XXX B) Papyrus of Ani	14
3. The Eater of the Dead. Papyrus of Ani	15
4. The Speech of Thoth. ,,	15
5. The Speech of the Gods ,,	15
6. The Speech of Horus ,,	16
7. The Speech of Ani ,,	16

III. The Chapters of Coming Forth by Day:

Chap. I. [hieroglyphs] Papyrus of Ani ... 18

Addition from the Turin Papyrus 21

Chap. I B. A. [hieroglyphs] Papyrus of Nekhtu-Ámen 23

Chap. I B. B. [hieroglyphs] Papyrus of Iuâu 25

Chap. II A. [hieroglyphs] Papyrus of Nu 26

	PAGE
Chap. II B. ... Papyrus of Ani	27
Chap. III. ... Papyrus of Nu ...	27
Chap. IV. ... Papyrus of Nu	28
Chap. V A. ... Papyrus of Nu	29
Chap. V B. ... Papyrus of Ani	29
Chap. VI A. ... Papyrus of Nu	29
Chap. VI B. ... Papyrus of Nebseni ...	30
Chap. VII. ... Papyrus of Nu	30
Chap. VIII A. ... Papyrus of Nu	31
Chap. VIII B. ... Papyrus of Ani	32

LIST OF CHAPTERS.   XXXV

PAGE

Chap. IX. [hieroglyphs] Papyrus of Ani 32

Chap. X. [hieroglyphs] Papyrus of Ani ... 33

Chap. XI. [hieroglyphs] Papyrus of Nu 33

Chap. XII. [hieroglyphs] Turin Papyrus ... 34

Chap. XIII. [hieroglyphs] Papyrus of Nebseni 35

Chap. XIV. [hieroglyphs] Papyrus of Mes-em-neter 35

Chap. XV. [hieroglyphs] Papyrus of Ani 36

Chap. XV. [hieroglyphs] Papyrus of Ani 38

Chap. XV. [hieroglyphs] Papyrus of Ani 40

c*

XXXVI   THE BOOK OF THE DEAD.

PAGE

Chap. XV. ... Papyrus of Mut-ḥetep 45

Chap. XV. ... Papyrus at Dublin 48

Chap. XVI. Vignettes only 50

Chap. XVII. 1. ... Papyrus of Iuâu 52

Chap. XVII. 2.

LIST OF CHAPTERS. XXXVII

PAGE

[hieroglyphs] Papyrus of Nebseni 53

Chap. XVII. 3. [hieroglyphs] Papyrus of Ani 84

Chap. XVIII. Introduction. Papyrus of Ani ... 96

Chap. XVIII A. [hieroglyphs] Papyri of Nebseni and Ani 97

Chap. XVIII B. [hieroglyphs] Coffin of Pa-neḥem-Ȧst 103

Chap. XIX A. [hieroglyphs] Papyrus of Netchemet 104

Chap. XIX B. [hieroglyphs] Turin Papyrus 109

Chap. XIX C. [hieroglyphs] Coffin of Pa-neḥem-Ȧst 112

XXXVIII   THE BOOK OF THE DEAD.

		PAGE
Chap. XX A. ⟨hieroglyphs⟩ Papyrus of Nebseni	...	115
Chap. XX B. ⟨hieroglyphs⟩ Turin Papyrus	...	118
Chap. XXI. ⟨hieroglyphs⟩ Papyrus of Nu	...	118
Chap. XXII. ⟨hieroglyphs⟩ Papyrus of Ani	...	119
Chap. XXIII. ⟨hieroglyphs⟩ Papyrus of Ani	...	120
Chap. XXIV. ⟨hieroglyphs⟩ Papyrus of Ani	...	120
Chap. XXV. ⟨hieroglyphs⟩ Papyrus of Nu	...	121
Chap. XXVI. ⟨hieroglyphs⟩ Papyrus of Ani	...	122
Chap. XXVII. ⟨hieroglyphs⟩ Papyrus of Ani	...	123
Chap. XXVIII. ⟨hieroglyphs⟩ Papyrus of Nu	...	124

LIST OF CHAPTERS XXXIX

PAGE

Chap. XXIX. 1. [hieroglyphs] Papyrus of Ani ... 125

Chap. XXIX. 2. [hieroglyphs] etc. Papyrus of Nu 126

Chap. XXIX A. [hieroglyphs] Papyrus of Ȧmen-ḥetep 126

Chap. XXIX B. [hieroglyphs] Papyrus of Ani 127

Chap. XXX. [hieroglyphs] Turin Papyrus ... 127

Chap. XXX A. [hieroglyphs] etc. Papyrus of Nu 128

Chap. XXX B. 1. [hieroglyphs] Papyrus of Ani 129

Chap. XXX B. 2. [hieroglyphs] Papyrus of Nu 130

Rubrics. From the Papyri of Nu and Ȧmen-ḥetep 131

Chap. XXXI. [hieroglyphs] Papyrus of Nu 132

XL   THE BOOK OF THE DEAD.

PAGE

Chap. XXXII. [hieroglyphs] Turin Papyrus   132

Chap. XXXIII. [hieroglyphs] Papyrus of Nu   134

Chap. XXXIV. [hieroglyphs] etc. Papyrus of Nu   135

Chap. XXXV. [hieroglyphs] Papyrus of Nu   135

Chap. XXXVI. [hieroglyphs] Papyrus of Nu   136

Chap. XXXVII. [hieroglyphs] Papyrus of Nu   136

Chap. XXXVIII A. [hieroglyphs] Papyrus of Nebseni   137

Chap. XXXVIII B. [hieroglyphs] Papyrus of Nu   138

Chap. XXXIX. [hieroglyphs] Papyrus of Mes-em-neter   139

Chap. XL A. [hieroglyphs] Papyrus of Nu   142

LIST OF CHAPTERS. XLI

PAGE

Chap. XL B. [hieroglyphs]
Papyrus of Rā 143

Chap. XLI. [hieroglyphs]
Papyrus of Nebseni 144

Chap. XLII. [hieroglyphs]
Papyrus of Nu 146

Chap. XLII. Section in tabular form. Papyrus of Ani 150

Chap. XLIII A. [hieroglyphs] Papyrus of Nu 154

Chap. XLIII B. [hieroglyphs] Papyrus of Ani 154

Chap. XLIV. [hieroglyphs] Papyrus of Ani 155

Chap. XLV. [hieroglyphs]
Papyrus of Ani 155

Chap. XLVI A. [hieroglyphs] Papyrus of Nebseni 156

Chap. XLVI B. [hieroglyphs] Papyrus of Nu 156

	PAGE
Chap. XLVI c. [hieroglyphs] Papyrus of Ani	156
Chap. XLVII. [hieroglyphs] etc. Papyrus of Nu	157
Chap. XLVIII. See Chapter X	33
Chap. XLIX. See Chapter XI	33
Chap. L A. [hieroglyphs] Papyrus of Nebseni	157
Chap. L B. [hieroglyphs] Papyrus of Nu	158
Chap. LI. [hieroglyphs] Papyrus of Nu	159
Chap. LII A. [hieroglyphs] Papyrus of Nu	159
Chap. LII B. [hieroglyphs] Papyrus of Nu	160
Chap. LIII. [hieroglyphs] Papyrus of Nu	164

LIST OF CHAPTERS. XLIII

	PAGE
Chap. LIV. [hieroglyphs] etc. Papyrus of Nu	166
Chap. LV. [hieroglyphs] Papyrus of Nu	166
Chap. LVI. [hieroglyphs] Papyrus of Nu	167
Chap. LVII. [hieroglyphs] Papyrus of Nu	167
Chap. LVII. Variant passage. Papyrus of Nefer-uben-f	169
Chap. LVIII. [hieroglyphs] Papyrus of Ani	169
Chap. LIX. [hieroglyphs] Papyrus of Ani	170
Chap. LX. [hieroglyphs] Turin Papyrus	171
Chap. LXI. [hieroglyphs] Papyrus of Ani	171
Chap. LXII A. [hieroglyphs] Papyrus of Nebseni	172
Chap. LXII B. [hieroglyphs] Papyrus of Nefer-uben-f	172

XLIV THE BOOK OF THE DEAD.

	PAGE
Chap. LXIII A. 1. [hieroglyphs] Papyrus of Nu	173
Chap. LXIII A. 2. [hieroglyphs] Papyrus of Iuâu	173
Chap. LXIII B. [hieroglyphs] Papyrus of Nu ...	174

Chap. LXIV. LONG VERSION:

1. [hieroglyphs] Papyrus of Nu   176
2. [hieroglyphs] Papyrus of Nebseni ...   177
3. [hieroglyphs] Papyrus of Iuâu   189

Chap. LXIV. SHORT VERSION:

1. [hieroglyphs] Papyrus of Nu ...   194
2. [hieroglyphs] Papyrus of Iuâu ...   195

LIST OF CHAPTERS. XLV

Volume II.

	PAGE
Chap. LXV A. Papyrus of Nu	1
Chap. LXV B. Turin Papyrus	3
Chap. LXVI. Papyrus of Åmen-em-ḥeb	3
Chap. LXVII. Papyrus of Nu	4
Chap. LXVIII. Papyrus of Nu	5
Chap. LXIX. Papyrus of Mes-em-neter	7
Chap. LXX. Papyrus of Mes-em-neter	9
Chap. LXXI. Papyrus of Nebseni	10
Chap. LXXII. Papyrus of Nebseni	15
Chap. LXXIII. Turin Papyrus	16
Chap. LXXIV. Papyrus of Nu	17

		PAGE
Chap. LXXV. [hieroglyphs] Papyrus of Nu		17
Chap. LXXVI. [hieroglyphs] Papyrus of Nu		18
Chap. LXXVII. [hieroglyphs] Papyrus of Nu		19
Chap. LXXVIII A. [hieroglyphs] Papyrus of Nu		21
Chap. LXXVIII B. [hieroglyphs] Papyrus of Ani		28
Chap. LXXIX. [hieroglyphs] Papyrus of Nu		35
Chap. LXXX. [hieroglyphs] Papyrus of Ani		37
Chap. LXXXI A. 1. [hieroglyphs] Papyrus of Nu		38
Chap. LXXXI. 2. [hieroglyphs] Papyrus of Iuáu		39
Chap. LXXXI. 3. [hieroglyphs] Papyrus of Ani		39

LIST OF CHAPTERS. XLVII

	PAGE
Chap. LXXXI B. ⸺ Papyrus of Ani	39
Chap. LXXXII A. ⸺ Papyrus of Nu	40
Chap. LXXXII B. ⸺ Papyrus of Iuâu	42
Chap. LXXXIII. ⸺ Papyrus of Nu	43
Chap. LXXXIV. ⸺ Papyrus of Nu	44
Chap. LXXXV. ⸺ Papyrus of Nu	45
Chap. LXXXVI. ⸺ Papyrus of Nu	47
Chap. LXXXVII. ⸺ Papyrus of Nu	49
Chap. LXXXVIII. ⸺ Papyrus of Nu	50

	PAGE
Chap. LXXXIX A. ... Papyrus of Nu	50
Chap. LXXXIX B. ... Papyrus of Ani	51
Chap. XC. ... Papyrus of Nu	53
Chap. XCI A. ... etc. Papyrus of Nu	54
Chap. XCI B. ... Papyrus of Ani	55
Chap. XCII. ... Papyrus of Nebseni	55
Chap. XCIII A. ... Papyrus of Nu ...	57
Chap. XCIII B. ... Papyrus of Ani	58
Chap. XCIV. ... Papyrus of Nu	59
Chap. XCV. ... Papyrus of Nu	60

LIST OF CHAPTERS.   XLIX

PAGE

Chap. XCVI. [hieroglyphs] Papyrus of Nu 61

Chap. XCVII A. [hieroglyphs] Papyrus of Nu 61

Chap. XCVII B. [hieroglyphs] Papyrus of Nebseni 62

Chap. XCVIII. [hieroglyphs] Papyrus of Nu 63

Chap. XCIX A. [hieroglyphs] Papyrus of Iuâu 65

Chap. XCIX B. RUBRIC. Papyrus of Nu 69

Chap. XCIX C. [hieroglyphs] Papyrus of Nefer-uben-f 71

Chap. C. [hieroglyphs] Papyrus of Nu 76

Chap. CI A. [hieroglyphs] Papyrus of Nu 77

Chap. CI B. [hieroglyphs] etc. Papyrus of Iuâu ... 79

d

THE BOOK OF THE DEAD.

	PAGE
Chap. CI c. ⸻ Papyrus of Netchemet	81
Chap. CII. ⸻ Papyrus of Nu	83
Chap. CIII. ⸻ Papyrus of Nu	85
Chap. CIV A. ⸻ Papyrus of Nu	85
Chap. CIV B. ⸻ Papyrus of Nebseni	85
Chap. CIV c. ⸻ Papyrus of Iuàu	86
Chap. CV. ⸻ Papyrus of Nu ...	86
Chap. CVI. ⸻ etc. Papyrus of Nu	87
Chap. CVII. ⸻ Turin Papyrus ...	88
Chap. CVIII. ⸻ Papyrus of Nu	89
Chap. CIX. ⸻ Papyrus of Nu	91

LIST OF CHAPTERS.

LI

PAGE

Chap. CX A. ... Papyrus of Nebseni ... 92

Chap. CX B. ... Papyrus of Iuàu 99

Chap. CXI. ... See Chapter CVIII. 89

Chap. CXII. ... Papyrus of Nu 105

Chap. CXIII. ... Papyrus of Nu 107

Chap. CXIV. ... Papyrus of Nebseni 109

Chap. CXV. ... Papyrus of Nu ... 110

Chap. CXVI. ... Papyrus of Nu 111

Chap. CXVII. ... Papyrus of Nu 112

Chap. CXVIII. ... Papyrus of Nu 113

d*

	PAGE
Chap. CXIX. [hieroglyphs] Papyrus of Nu	113
Chap. CXX. See Chapter XII. Turin Papyrus	34
Chap. CXXI. See Chapter XIII. Papyrus of Nebseni	35
Chap. CXXII. [hieroglyphs] Papyrus of Nu	114
Chap. CXXIII. [hieroglyphs] Papyrus of Nu	115
Chap. CXXIV. [hieroglyphs] or [hieroglyphs] Papyrus of Nu	116
Chap. CXXV. INTRODUCTION:	
A. [hieroglyphs] Papyrus of Ani	119
B. [hieroglyphs] etc. [hieroglyphs] Papyrus of Nu	121
Chap. CXXV. NEGATIVE CONFESSION:	
A. [hieroglyphs] Papyrus of Nebseni	124
B. [hieroglyphs] Papyrus of Nu ...	125
C. [hieroglyphs] Papyrus of Iuáu ...	126
D. [hieroglyphs] Papyrus of Ani ...	127

LIST OF CHAPTERS.

PAGE

Chap. CXXV. ADDRESS TO THE GODS:
- A. [hieroglyphs] Papyrus of Nu 140
- B. [hieroglyphs] Papyrus of Iuȧu 147

Chap. CXXVI. [hieroglyphs] Papyrus of Nu 155

Chap. CXXVII A. [hieroglyphs] Tomb of Rameses IV 156

Chap. CXXVII B. [hieroglyphs] Papyrus of Ptaḥ-mes 159

Chap. CXXVIII. [hieroglyphs] Turin Papyrus 161

Chap. CXXIX. [hieroglyphs] Turin Papyrus 163

Chap. CXXX. [hieroglyphs] Papyrus of Nu 164

Chap. CXXXI. [hieroglyphs] Papyrus of Nu 171

Chap. CXXXII. [hieroglyphs] Papyrus of Ani 172

THE BOOK OF THE DEAD.

	PAGE
Chap. CXXXIII. ... Papyrus of Nu	173
Chap. CXXXIV. ... Papyrus of Nu	176
Chap. CXXXV. ... Turin Papyrus	179
Chap. CXXXVI. SHORT VERSION:	
A. ... Papyrus of Nu	180
B. ... Papyrus of Nebseni	180
C. ... Papyrus of Iuâu	181
Chap. CXXXVI. LONG VERSION:	
A. ... Papyrus of Nu	181
B. ... Papyrus of Nu	185
Chap. CXXXVII A. 1. ... Papyrus of Nu ...	187

LIST OF CHAPTERS. LV

PAGE

Chap. CXXXVII A. 2. [hieroglyphs] Papyrus of Nebseni 191

Chap. CXXXVII B. [hieroglyphs] Papyrus of Nebseni 198

Chap. CXXXVIII. [hieroglyphs] Papyrus of Nu 198

Chap. CXXXIX A. [hieroglyphs] Papyrus of Netchemet 200

Chap. CXXXIX B. [hieroglyphs] Turin Papyrus 200

Chap. CXL. [hieroglyphs] Turin Papyrus 201

Chap. CXLI. [hieroglyphs] Papyrus of Nu 203

Chap. CXLII A. THE FORMS OF OSIRIS, etc. Papyrus of Nu 206

Chap. CXLII B. THE FORMS OF OSIRIS, etc. Papyrus of Iuàu 209

Chap. CXLII c. THE FORMS OF OSIRIS, etc. Papyrus of Ȧmen-ḥetep 210

Chap. CXLII D. THE FORMS OF OSIRIS, etc. Turin Papyrus 212

	PAGE
Chap. CXLIII. Vignettes only	218
Chap. CXLIV A. THE SEVEN ĀRITS. Papyrus of Nu	218
Chap. CXLIV B. THE SEVEN ĀRITS. Papyrus of Iuȧu	218

Chap. CXLV. [hieroglyphs] Turin Papyrus:

FIRST PYLON [hieroglyphs]	... ...	224
SECOND PYLON [hieroglyphs]	... ...	225
THIRD PYLON [hieroglyphs]	... ...	226
FOURTH PYLON [hieroglyphs]	... ...	226
FIFTH PYLON [hieroglyphs]	... ...	227
SIXTH PYLON [hieroglyphs]	... ...	227
SEVENTH PYLON [hieroglyphs]	... ...	228
EIGHTH PYLON [hieroglyphs]	... ...	229
NINTH PYLON [hieroglyphs]	... ...	229
TENTH PYLON [hieroglyphs]	... ...	230
ELEVENTH PYLON [hieroglyphs]	...	231
TWELFTH PYLON [hieroglyphs]	...	231
THIRTEENTH PYLON [hieroglyphs]	...	231

LIST OF CHAPTERS.

	PAGE
Fourteenth Pylon [hieroglyphs]	232
Fifteenth Pylon [hieroglyphs]	233
Sixteenth Pylon [hieroglyphs]	233
Seventeenth Pylon [hieroglyphs]	233
Eighteenth Pylon [hieroglyphs]	234
Nineteenth Pylon [hieroglyphs]	234
Twentieth Pylon [hieroglyphs]	235
Twenty-first Pylon [hieroglyphs]	235

Chap. CXLVI A. [hieroglyphs] Papyrus of Nu ... 238

Chap. CXLVI B. [hieroglyphs] Papyrus of Iuâu 244

Chap. CXLVI c. [hieroglyphs] Papyrus of Ḥeru-em-khebit 247

Chap. CXLVI. Text from the Saïte Recension 249

Chap. CXLVII. Papyrus of Ani and Papyrus of Ḥeru-em-khebit:

[hieroglyphs] 253

[hieroglyphs] 253

LVIII   THE BOOK OF THE DEAD.

	PAGE
[hieroglyphs]	254
[hieroglyphs]	254
[hieroglyphs]	255
[hieroglyphs]	255
[hieroglyphs]	256

Chap. CXLVIII A. [hieroglyphs] Papyrus of Nu 261

Chap. CXLVIII B. [hieroglyphs] Papyrus of Ani 264

Chap. CXLVIII c. Introduction and text [hieroglyphs] Papyrus of Netchemet 267

Chap. CL. The Domains of Osiris. Papyrus of Nu:

First Domain [hieroglyphs]	... ...	270
Second Domain [hieroglyphs]	... ...	270
Third Domain [hieroglyphs]	... ...	272
Fourth Domain [hieroglyphs]	... ...	272
Fifth Domain [hieroglyphs]	... ...	273
Sixth Domain [hieroglyphs]	... ...	274

LIST OF CHAPTERS. LIX

	PAGE
SEVENTH DOMAIN	275
EIGHTH DOMAIN	275
NINTH DOMAIN	276
TENTH DOMAIN	277
ELEVENTH DOMAIN	278
TWELFTH DOMAIN	279
THIRTEENTH DOMAIN	280
FOURTEENTH DOMAIN	281
Chap. CL. The Names of the Domains of Osiris	282
Chap. CLI A. Papyrus of Mut-ḥetep	283
Chap. CLI B. Papyrus of Nebseni	286
Chap. CLI c. Papyrus of Iuâu	289
Chap. CLII. Papyrus of Nu	290

lx   THE BOOK OF THE DEAD

Volume III.

		PAGE
Chap. CLIII A. Papyrus of Nu	... ...	1
Chap. CLIII B. Papyrus of Nu	... ...	6
Chap. CLIV A. Papyrus of Nu	... ...	9
Chap. CLIV B. Turin Papyrus	... ...	12
Chap. CLV A. Papyrus of Nu	...	14
Chap. CLV B. Papyrus of Iuâu		15
Chap. CLV c. Rubric. Turin Papyrus	... ...	15
Chap. CLVI A. Papyrus of Nu		16
Chap. CLVI B. Papyrus of Iuâu	... ...	17
Chap. CLVI c. Turin Papyrus		17
Chap. CLVII. Turin Papyrus	... ...	18
Chap. CLVIII. Turin Papyrus	... ...	19

LIST OF CHAPTERS. LXI

PAGE

Chap. CLIX. Turin Papyrus 19

Chap. CLX. Papyrus of Nebseni 20

Chap. CLXI. Papyrus of Nefer-uben-f 21

Chap. CLXII. Turin Papyrus 22

Chap. CLXIII. Turin Papyrus 24

Chap. CLXIV. Turin Papyrus 28

Chap. CLXV. Turin Papyrus 31

Chap. CLXVI. Papyrus of Nebseni 33

Chap. CLXVII. Papyrus of Nebseni 34

Chap. CLXVIII A. Papyrus of Mut-ḥetep 34

Chap. CLXVIII B. Papyrus No. 10,478 36

		PAGE
Chap. CLXIX. [hieroglyphs] Papyrus of Nefer-uben-f	...	47
Chap. CLXX. [hieroglyphs] Papyrus of Nefer-uben-f	...	51
Chap. CLXXI. [hieroglyphs] Papyrus of Ȧmen-ḥetep	...	53
Chap. CLXXII. [hieroglyphs] Papyrus of Nebseni	...	54
Chap. CLXXIII. [hieroglyphs] Papyrus of Nebseni	...	62
Chap. CLXXIV. [hieroglyphs] Papyrus of Mut-ḥetep	...	67
Chap. CLXXV. [hieroglyphs] Papyrus of Mut-ḥetep	...	72
Chap. CLXXVI. [hieroglyphs] Papyrus of Ani	...	78

LIST OF CHAPTERS. LXIII

	PAGE
Chap. CLXXVII. [hieroglyphs] Papyrus of Nebseni ...	80
Chap. CLXXVIII. [hieroglyphs] Papyrus of Nebseni	81
Chap. CLXXVIII. Ancient version from the Pyramid of Unás	86
Chap. CLXXIX. [hieroglyphs] Papyrus of Nu	90
Chap. CLXXX. [hieroglyphs] From a Papyrus at Paris	92
Chap. CLXXXI. [hieroglyphs] Papyrus of Qenna, p. 97, and Papyrus of Amen-em-ȧpt (at Rome)	99
Chap. CLXXXII. [hieroglyphs] Papyrus of Mut-ḥetep	101
Chap. CLXXXIII. [hieroglyphs] Papyrus of Hunefer	105

	PAGE
Chap. CLXXXIV. [Text wanting]	109
Chap. CLXXXV. [hieroglyphs] Papyrus of Sutimes	109
Chap. CLXXXVI. [hieroglyphs] Papyrus of Ani	110
Chap. CLXXXVII. [hieroglyphs] Papyrus of Nu	111
Chap. CLXXXVIII. [hieroglyphs] Papyrus of Nu	111
Chap. CLXXXIX. [See Vol. I, p. 160, Chapter LII B]	112
Chap. CXC [CXLVIII]. [hieroglyphs] Papyrus of Nu	112

Appendix I.

I. A PRAYER FOR THE PRESERVATION OF A PYRAMID-TOMB 116

II. THE CONTRACT BEETWEEN ÁMEN-RĀ AND NESI-KHENSU 117

III. THE BOOK OF BREATHINGS. Part I. [hieroglyphs] Papyrus of Ḳersher 133

LIST OF CHAPTERS. LXV

	PAGE
The Book of Breathings. Part II. [hieroglyphs] Papyrus at Rome	142
IV. The Book of Traversing Eternity. [hieroglyphs] Long Version. Papyrus at Vienna	150
The Book of Traversing Eternity. Short Version. Stele in the Vatican	157
V. Address to Takhert-p-seru-ȧbtiu. Papyrus in the British Museum, No. 10,112 ...	160
VI. A prayer for the Preservation of the Name. Pyramid of Pepi II	162
VII. Funeral Text of Hertu. Papyrus at Berlin	166
VIII. Funeral Text of Ānkh-f-en-ḥetemti. Papyrus at Cairo	175

Appendix II.

SPECIMEN CHAPTERS OF THE BOOK OF THE DEAD FROM RECENSIONS OF VARIOUS PERIODS.

A. I. Chap. XLII. From the Pyramid of Pepi I	184
A. II. 1. Chap. XVII. From the tomb of Ḥer ...	189
A. II. 2. Chap. XVII. From the sarcophagus of Ḥer	192
A. II. 3. Chap. XVII. From the sarcophagus of Ḥer	200
A. II. 4. Chap. XVII. From the coffin of Sat-Bast	205

	PAGE
A. II. 5. Chap. XXIV. Of bringing spells ...	210
A. II. 6. Chap. XXIX. Of not letting the heart of a man be carried away. Two Versions	211, 212
A. II. 7. Chap. XLIII. Of not letting the head of a man be cut off	212
A. II. 8, 9. Chap. LII. Of not eating filth. Two Versions	213, 214
A. II. 10. Chap. LIV. Of living in the air, of smelling the air	215
A. II. 11, 12. Chap. LXII. Of having power over water. Two Versions	217, 218
A. II. 13. Chap. XCIX. Of bringing a Boat ...	219
A. II. 14. Chap. ..... Of finding the Reḥti Goddesses	228
A. II. 15. Chap. ..... Of not being tripped up in the Other World	229
A. II. 16. Chap. ..... Of entering the Boat of Hathor	230
A. II. 17. Chap. ..... Of entering the Boat of Rā	231
A. II. 18. Chap. ..... Of remembering Words of Power	232
A. II. 19. Chap. ..... Of the recognition of Friends	234
A. II. 20. Chap. ..... Of journeying in peace in the House of Osiris	238
A. III. 1. Chap. XXVI. From the Stone of Peṭa-Àmen-àpt	241
A. III. 2. Chap. XXX B. From the Stone of Peṭa-Àmen-àpt	242

LIST OF CHAPTERS. LXVII

PAGE

A. III. 3. Chap. LXIV. From the Stone of Peṭā-
Ȧmen-àpt 243

Chapters from the Coffin of Basa-en-Mut in the
British Museum:

A. IV. 1. Chap. I 249

A. IV. 2. Chap. II ... 253

A. IV. 3. Chap. IX ... 254

A. IV. 4. Chap. X 256

A. IV. 5. Chap. XXIII 257

A. IV. 6. Chap. XXIV ... 257

A. IV. 7. Chap. XXVI ... 258

A. IV. 8. Chap. XXVIII 259

A. IV. 9. Chap. XXX B ... 260

A. IV. 10. Chap. XXXI ... 260

A. IV. 11. Chap. XLIV ... 262

A. IV. 12. Chap. XLVII 263

A. IV. 13. Chap. LVI 263

A. IV. 14. Chap. LIX 264

e*

LXVIII THE BOOK OF THE DEAD.

		PAGE
A. IV. 15.	Chap. LXIII A	264
A. IV. 16.	Chap. LXVIII	265
A. IV. 17.	Chap. LXXI	267
A. IV. 18.	Chap. LXXXIX	269
A. IV. 19.	Chap. XCI	270
A. IV. 20.	Chap. CV	270
A. IV. 21.	Chap. CLIV	271
A. IV. 22.	Addresses to the gods	274
B. I.	Funerary Text of Queen Ānkh-nes-nefer-āb-Rā	277
B. II.	Saïte Version of a text from the Pyramid of Unȧs	294

THE CHAPTERS
OF
COMING FORTH BY DAY.

Introductory Hymn to Rā, the Sun-god.
[From the Papyrus of Ani (Brit. Mus. No. 10,470, sheet 1).]

THE BOOK OF THE DEAD.

HYMNS TO RĀ BY ANI AND QENNA.

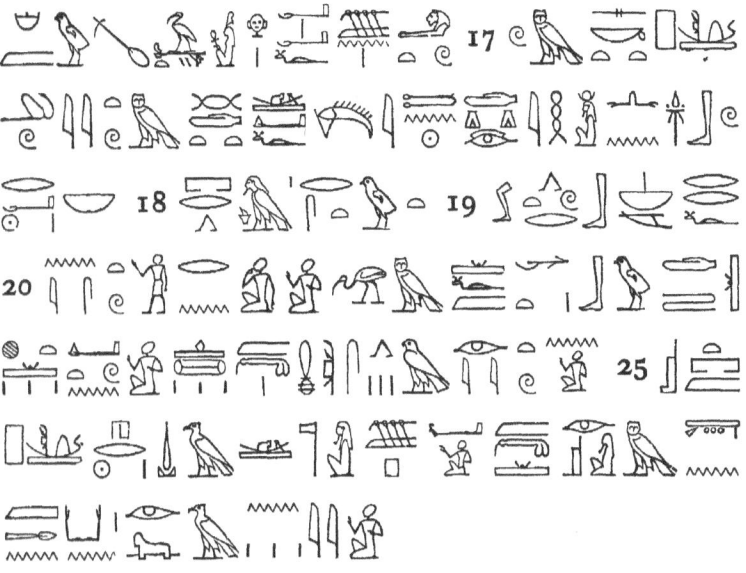

Introductory Hymn to Rā, the Sun-god.

[From the Papyrus of Qenna (see Leemans, *Papyrus Égyptien*, t. 2, plate 2).]

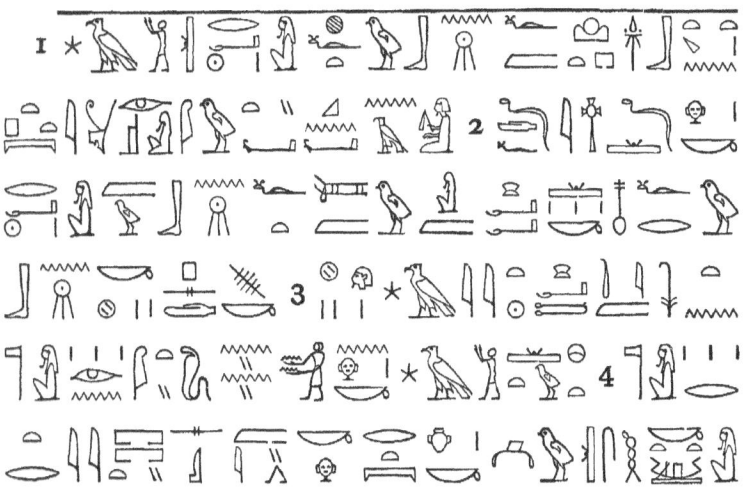

1*

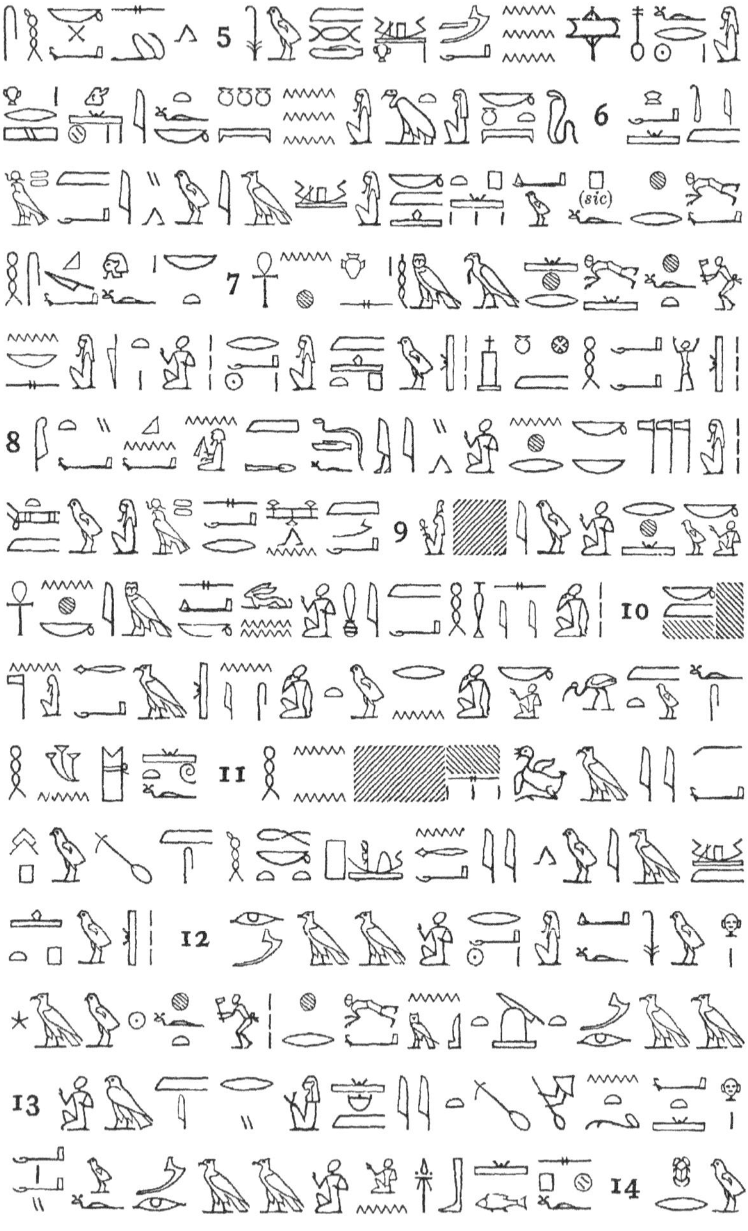

HYMN TO RĀ BY QENNA.

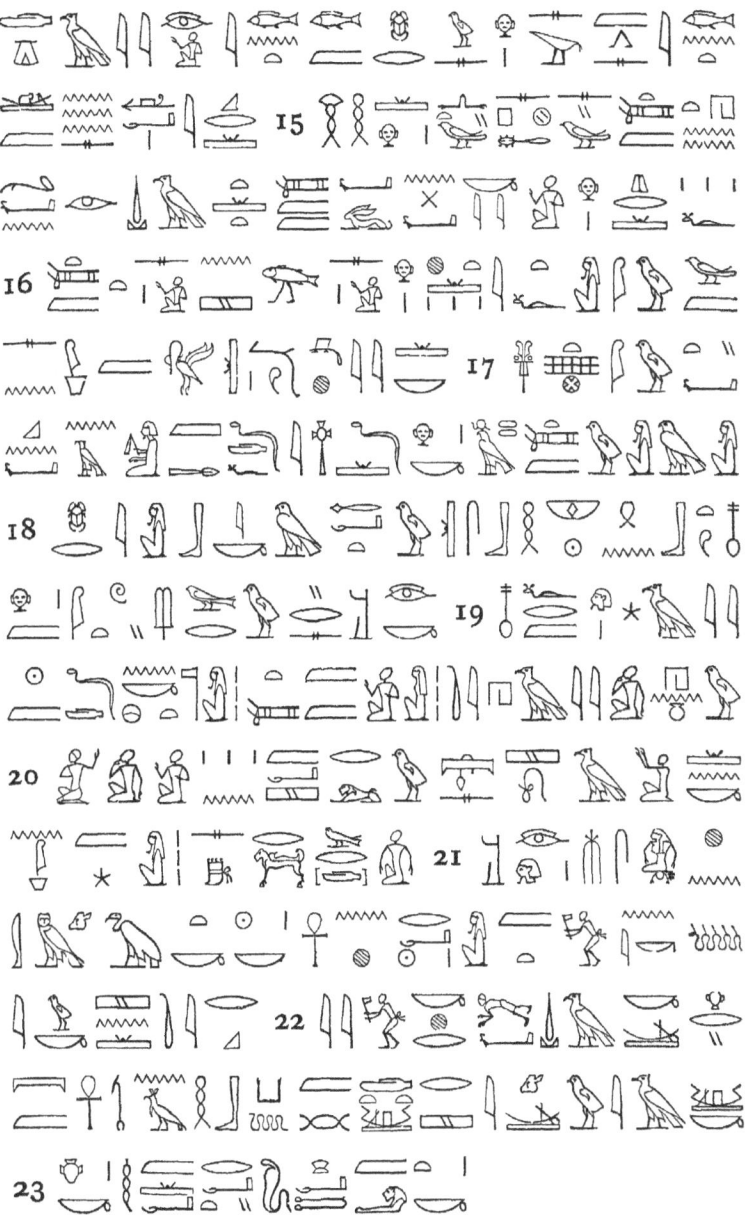

Introductory Hymn to Rā, the Sun-god.

[From the Papyrus of Qenna (see Leemans, *Papyrus Égyptien*, t. 2, plate 4).]

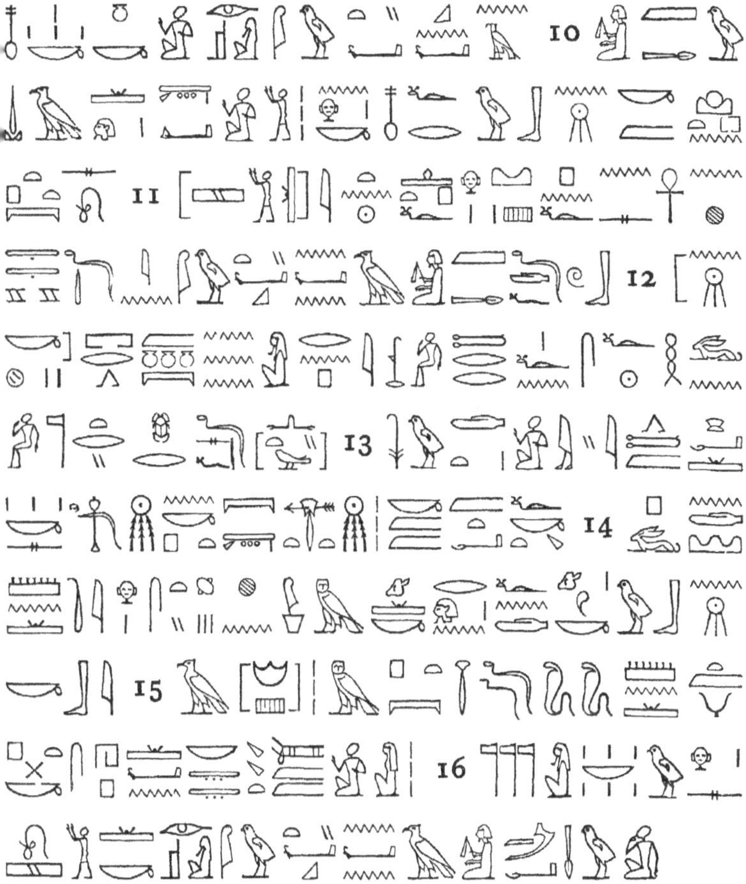

Introductory Hymn to Rā, the Sun-god.

[From the Papyrus of Hunefer (Brit. Mus. No. 9,901, sheet 1).]

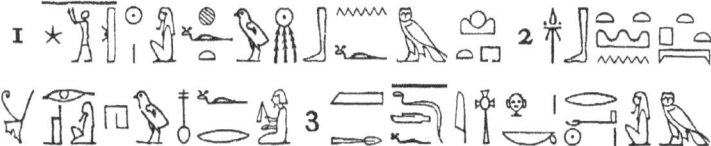

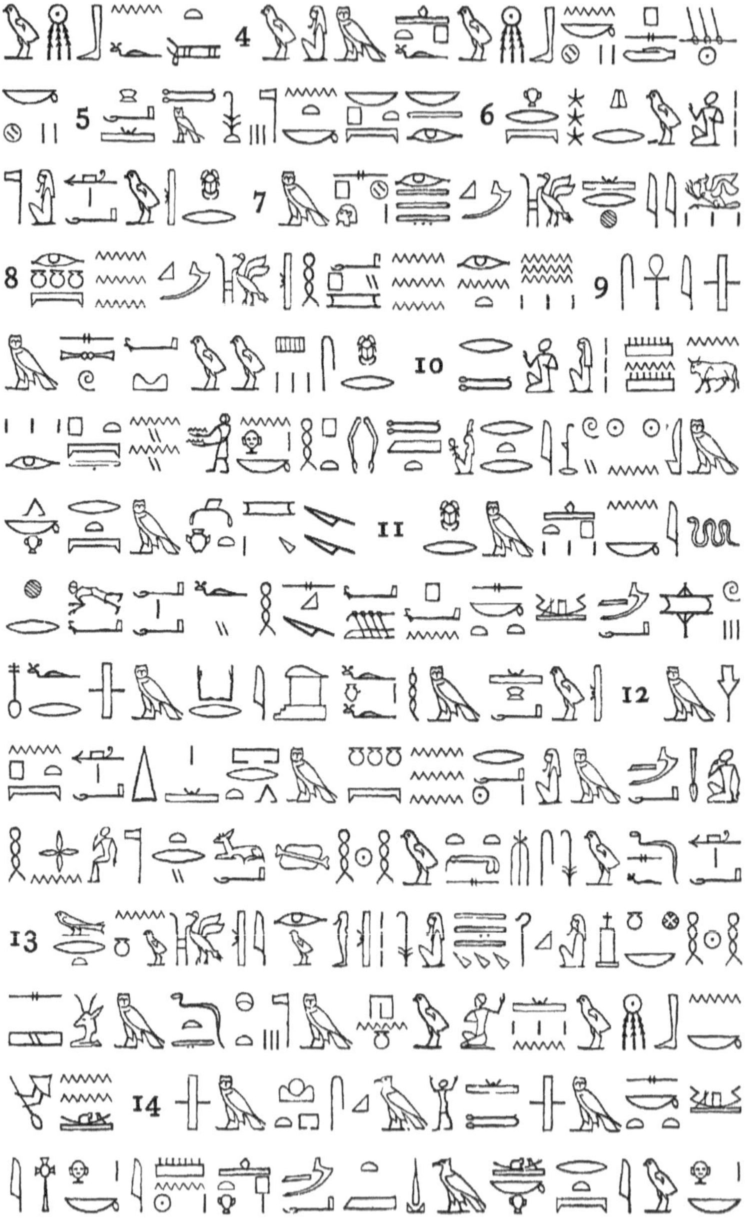

HYMN TO RĀ BY HUNEFER.

Introductory Hymn to Rā, the Sun-god.

[From the Papyrus of Nekht (Brit. Mus. No. 10,471, sheet 21).]

HYMN TO RĀ BY NEKHT.

Introductory Hymn to Osiris Un-Nefer.

[From the Papyrus of Ani (Brit. Mus. No. 10,470, sheet 2).]

THE SCENE OF THE JUDGMENT. 13

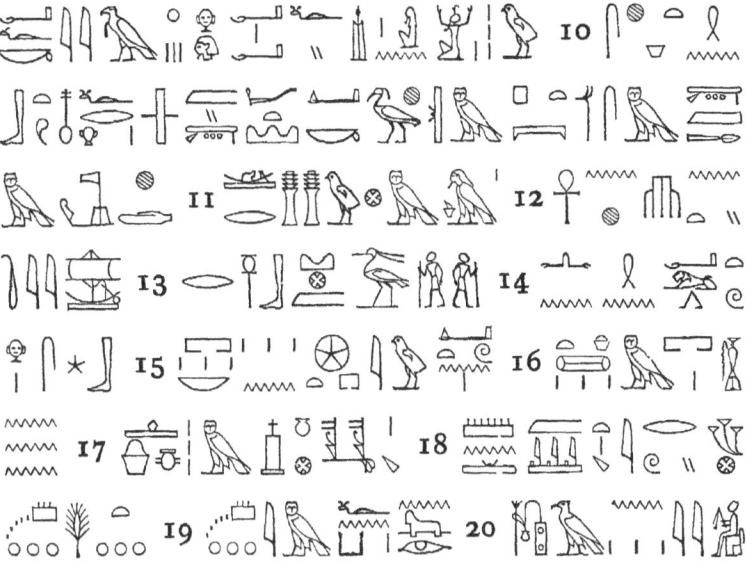

The Scene of the Weighing of the Heart of the Deceased.

[From the Papyrus of Ani (Brit. Mus. No. 10,470, sheets 3 and 4).]

I. NAMES OF THE GODS OF THE GREAT COMPANY:—

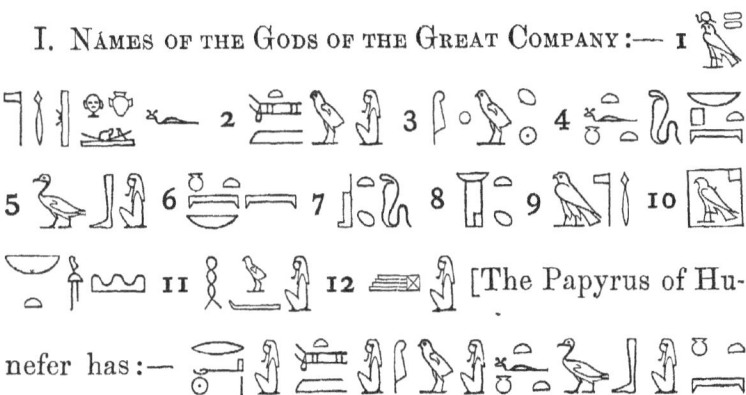

[The Papyrus of Hunefer has:—

II. The Prayer of the Deceased [Chapter XXX B]:—

THE SCENE OF THE JUDGMENT. 15

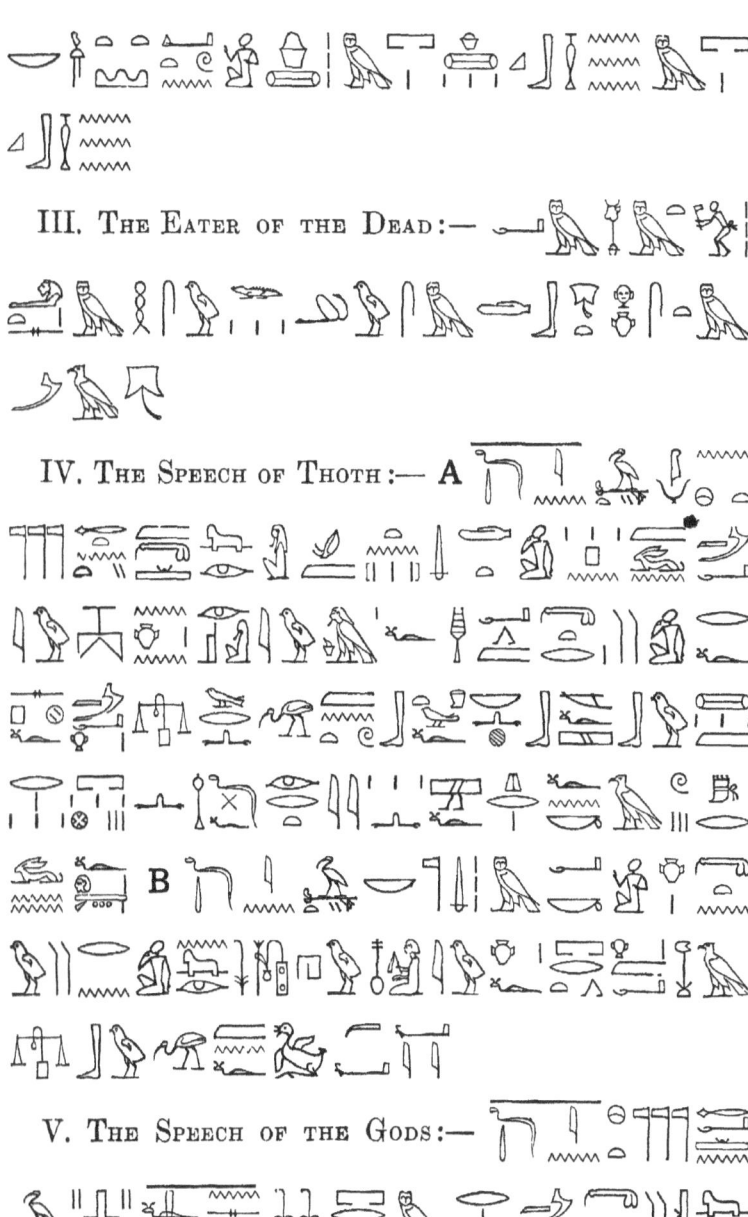

III. THE EATER OF THE DEAD:—

IV. THE SPEECH OF THOTH:— A

B

V. THE SPEECH OF THE GODS:—

16 THE BOOK OF THE DEAD.

VI. The Speech of Horus:—

VII. The Speech of Ani:—

THE SCENE OF THE JUDGMENT.

The Chapters of Coming Forth by Day.

Chapter I.

[From the Papyrus of Ani (Brit. Mus. No. 10,470, sheets 5 and 6).]

OF COMING FORTH BY DAY.

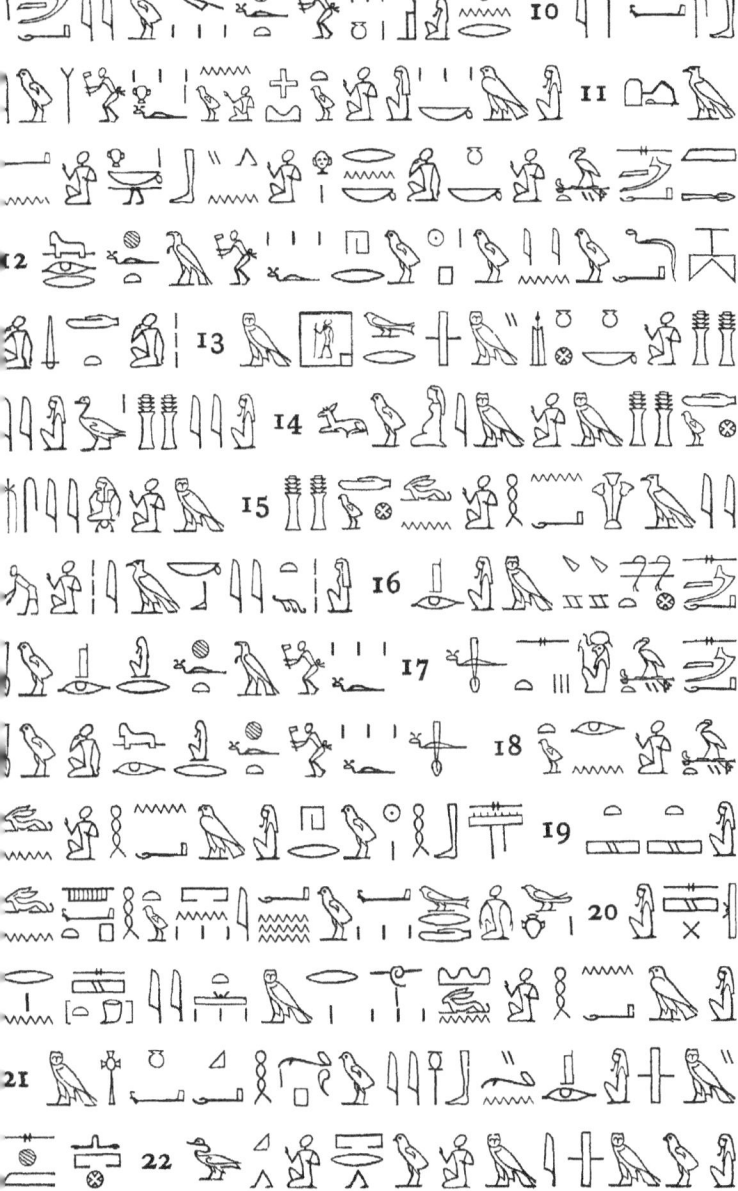

CHAP. I]   OF COMING FORTH BY DAY.   21

The Turin Papyrus (Lepsius, *Todtenbuch*, Bl. 1) adds:—

CHAP. I] OF MAKING THE SĀḤU ENTER THE ṬUAT. 23

CHAPTER I B.

[From the Papyrus of Nekhtu-Åmen (Naville, *Todtenbuch*, Bd. 1, Bl. 5).]

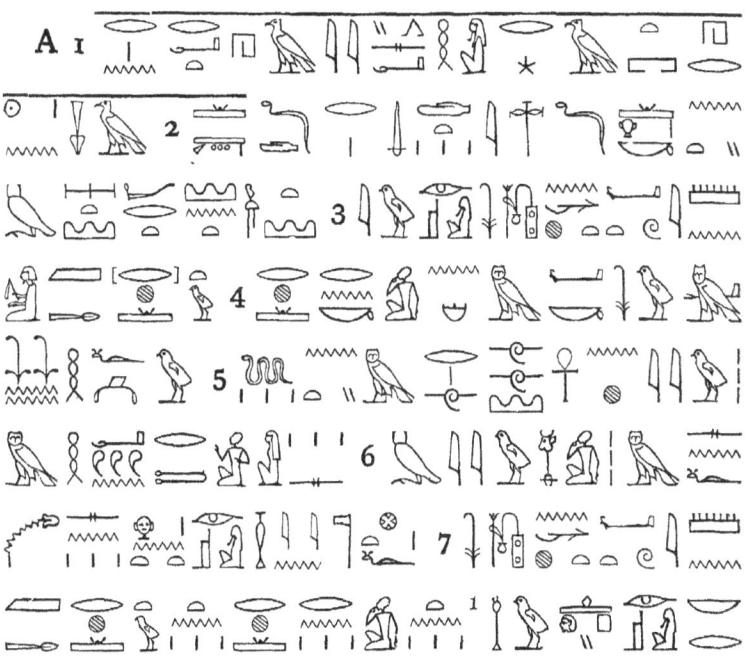

1. The names of the Nine Serpents are given in the DAVIS PAPYRUS of IUAU (ed. Naville, plate XIX); see version B of this Chapter on p. 25.

THE BOOK OF THE DEAD. [Chap. I B

CHAP. I B] OF MAKING THE SĀḤU ENTER THE ṬUAT.

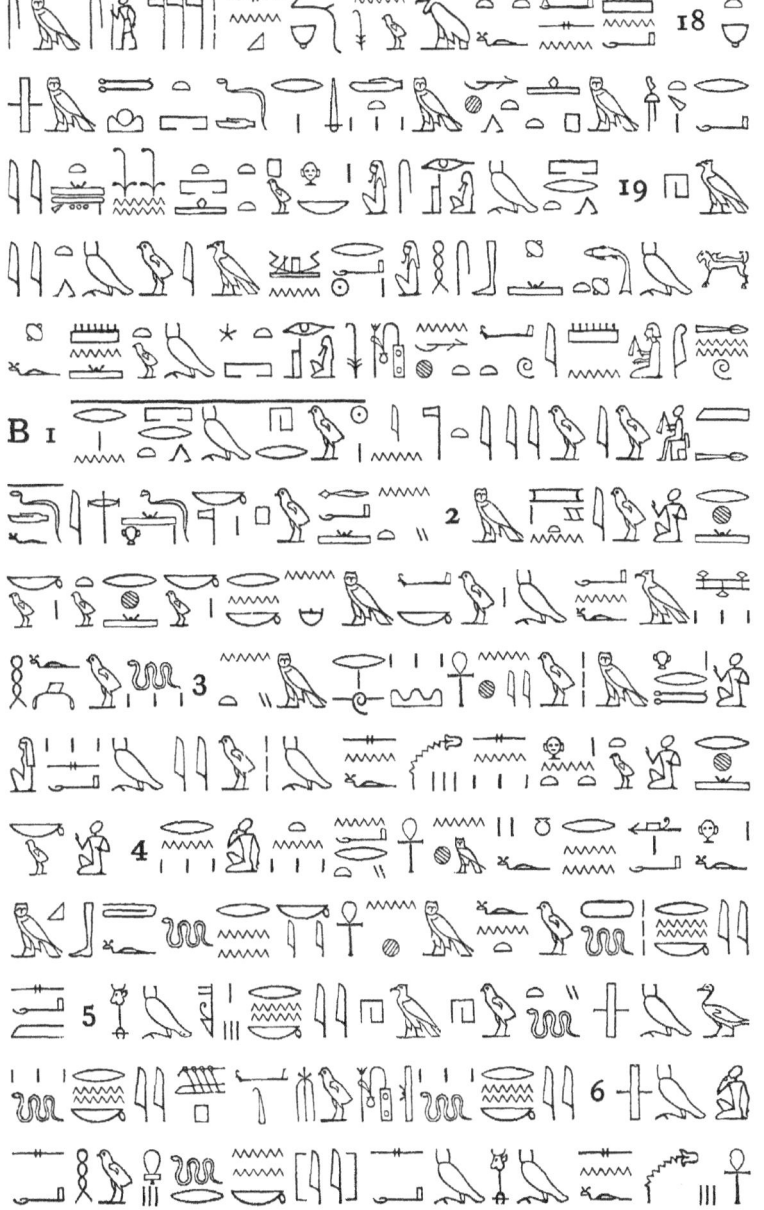

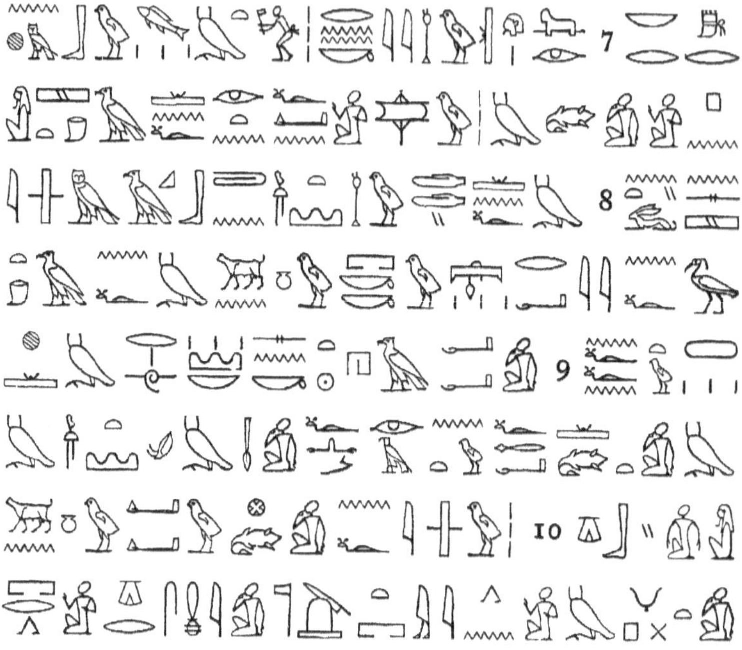

26 THE BOOK OF THE DEAD. [Chap. II

[End. Followed by pictures of the Nine Serpents.]

Chapter II.

[A. From the Papyrus of Nu (Brit. Mus. No. 10,477, sheet 13).]
[B. From the Papyrus of Ani (Brit Mus. No. 10,470, sheet 18).]

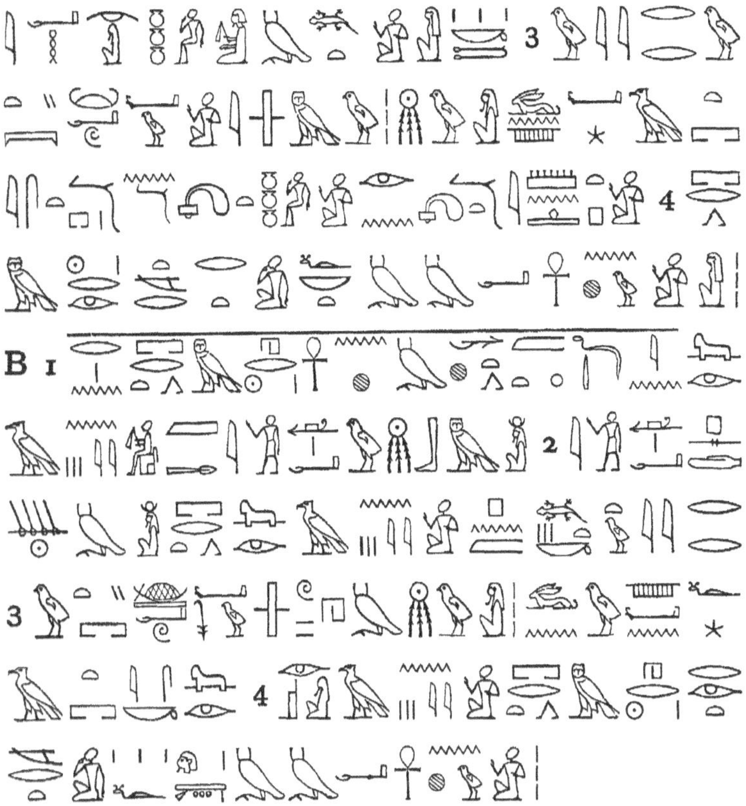

CHAP. III] OF LIVING AFTER DEATH. 27

[hieroglyphs]

CHAPTER III.

[From the Papyrus of Nu (Brit. Mus. No. 10,477, sheet 13)]

28   THE BOOK OF THE DEAD.   [Chap. IV

Chapter IV.

[From the Papyrus of Nu (Brit. Mus. No. 10,477, sheet 19).]

CHAPS. V, VI] OF NOT DOING WORK IN THE TUAT. 29

CHAPTER V.

[A. From the Papyrus of Nu (Brit. Mus. No. 10,477, sheet 21).]
[B. From the Papyrus of Nebseni (Brit. Mus. No. 9,900, sheet 11).]

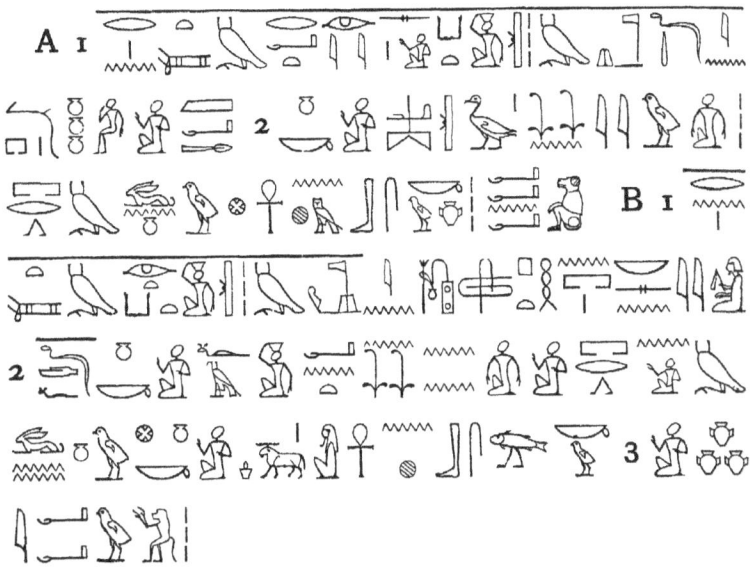

CHAPTER VI.

[A. From the Papyrus of Nu (Brit. Mus. No. 10,477, sheet 21).]
[B. From the Papyrus of Nebseni (Brit. Mus. No. 9,900, sheet 10).]

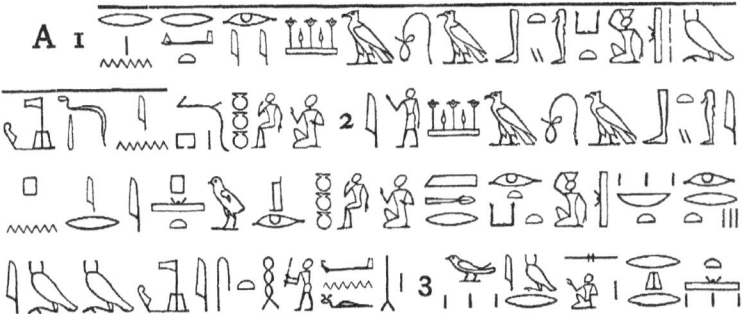

CHAPTER VII.

[From the Papyrus of Nu (Brit. Mus. No. 10,477, sheet 22).]

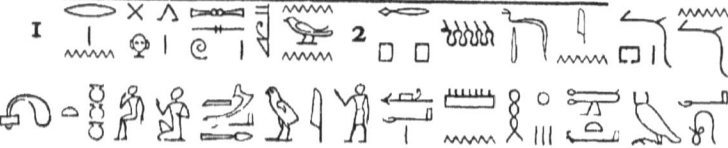

CHAP. VIII] OF ENTERING ÂMENT BY DAY. 31

Chapter VIII.

[A. From the Papyrus of Nu (Brit. Mus. No. 10,477, sheet 12).]
[B. From the Papyrus of Ani (Brit. Mus. No. 10,470, sheet 18).]

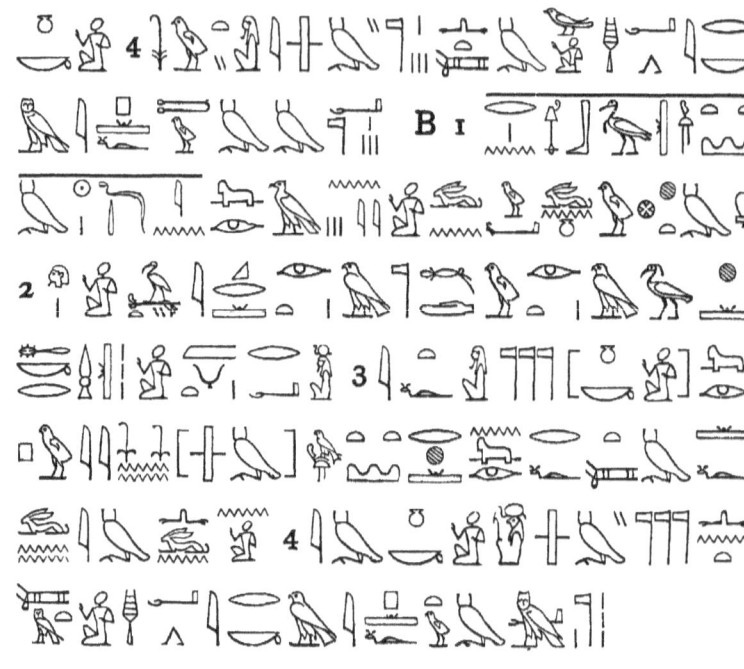

Chapter IX.

[From the Papyrus of Ani (Brit. Mus. No. 10,470, sheet 18).]

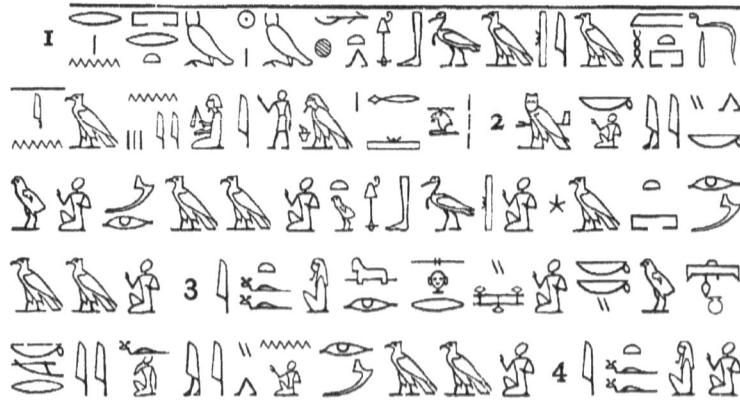

EGRESS AGAINST ENEMIES.

CHAPTER X.

[From the Papyrus of Ani (Brit. Mus. No. 10,470, sheet 18).]

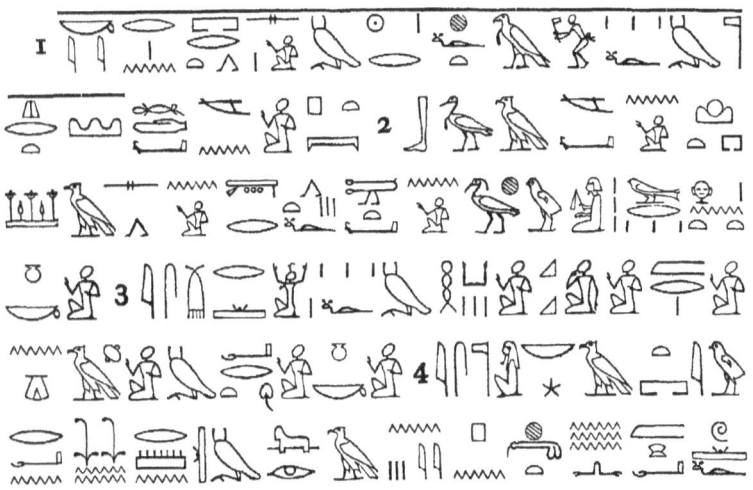

CHAPTER XI.

[From the Papyrus of Nu (Brit. Mus. No. 10,477, sheet 21).]

34 THE BOOK OF THE DEAD. [Chap. XII

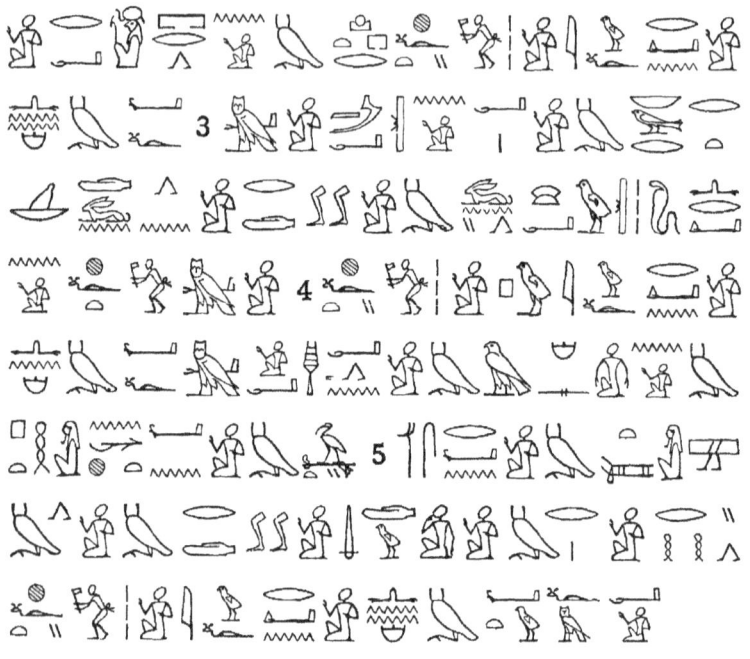

Chapter XII. (Saïte Recension, Chap. CXX.)
[From the Papyrus of Nu (Brit. Mus. No. 10,477, sheet 9).]

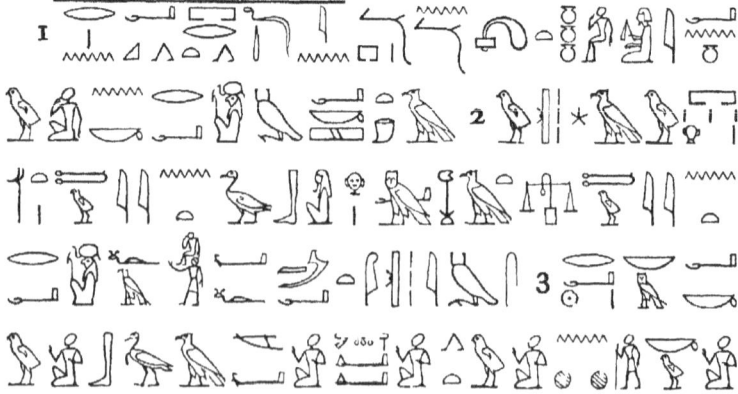

OF DESTROYING ANXIETY.

CHAPTER XIII. (Saïte Recension, Chap. CXXI.)

[From the Papyrus of Nebseni (Brit. Mus. No. 9,900, sheet 12, line 6).]

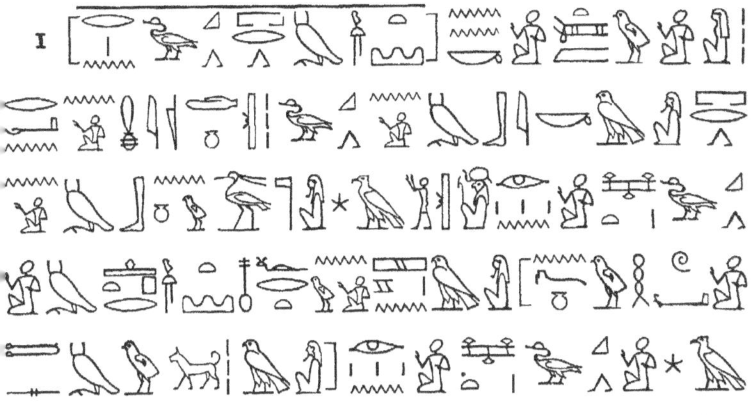

I [hieroglyphs]

RUBRIC. [hieroglyphs]

(Lepsius, *Todtenbuch*, Bll. 4, 45).

CHAPTER XIV.

[From the Papyrus of Mes-em-neter (Naville, *Todtenbuch*, Bd. I, Bl. 13).]

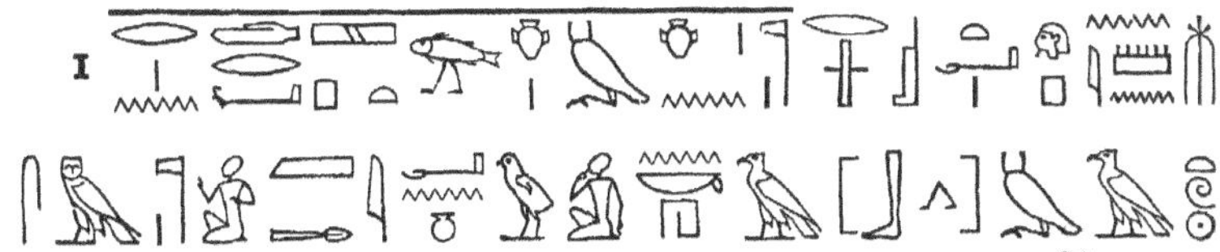

I [hieroglyphs]

Chapter XV.

Hymn to the rising and setting Sun.

[From the Papyrus of Ani (Brit. Mus. No. 10,470, sheets 18, 19).]

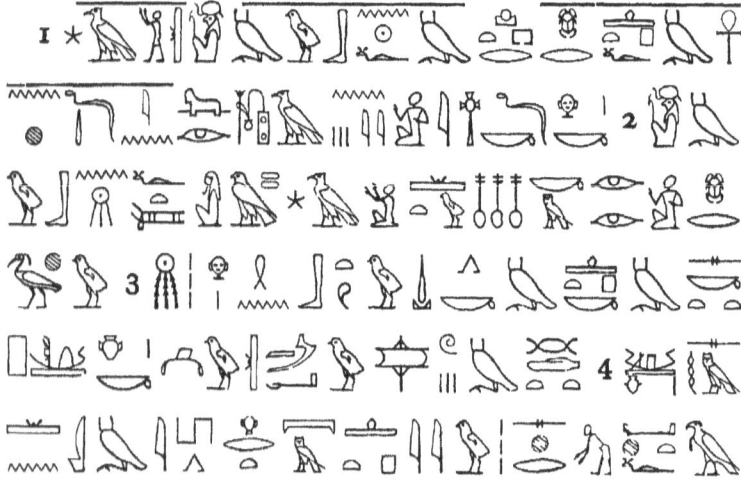

HYMN TO RĀ AT SUNRISE.

38 THE BOOK OF THE DEAD. [Chap. XV

Litany to Osiris.

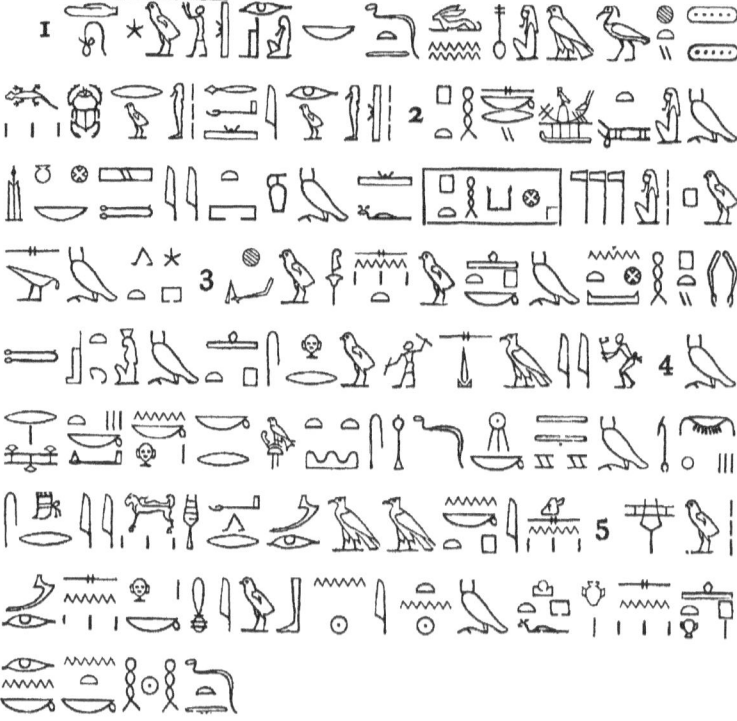

LITANY TO OSIRIS.

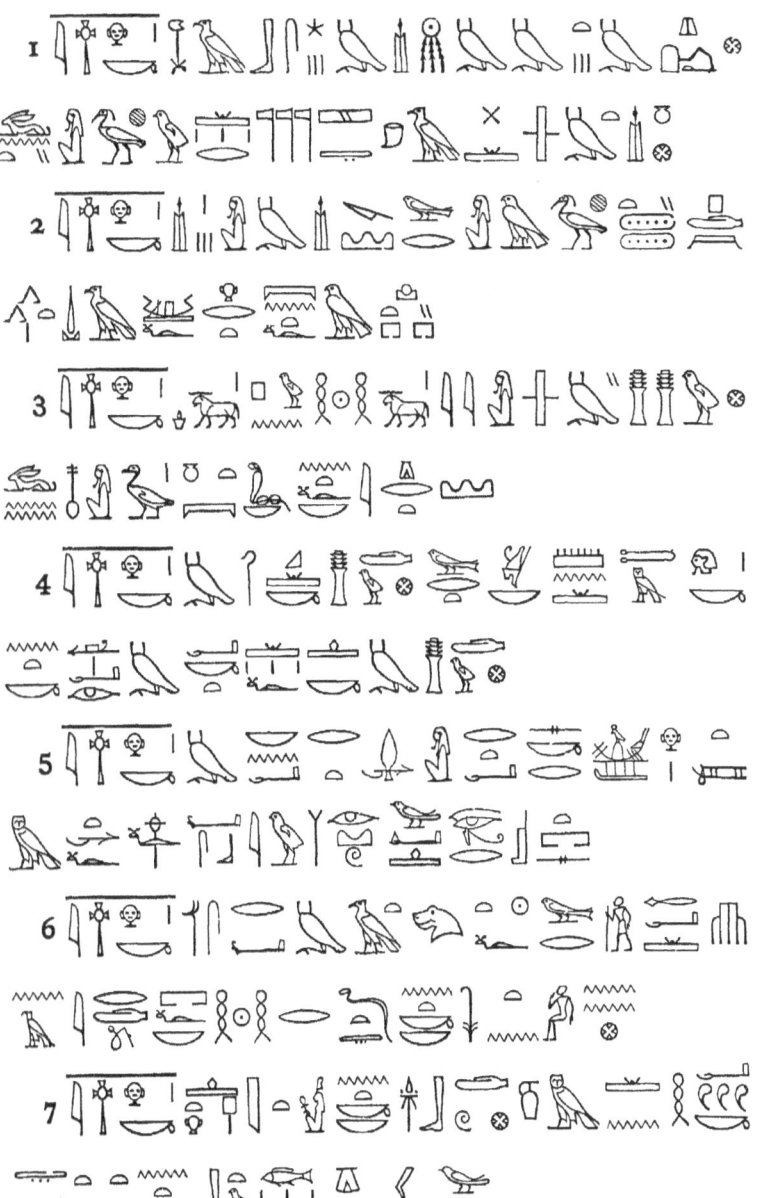

40 THE BOOK OF THE DEAD. [Chap. xv

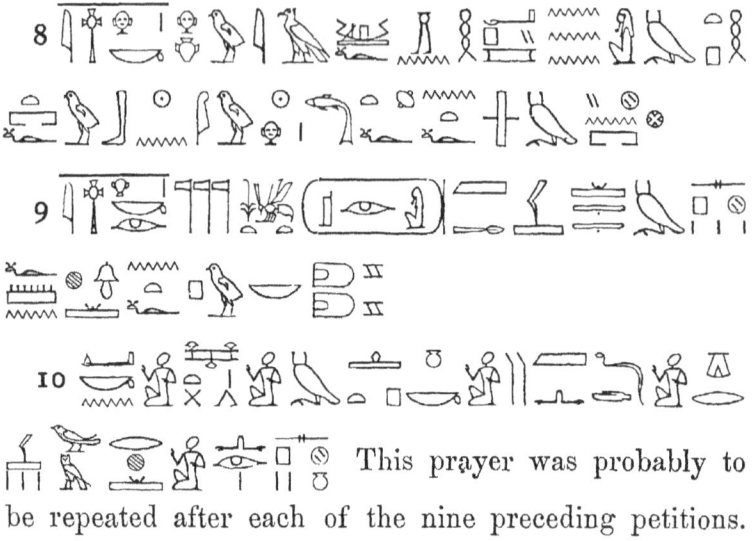 This prayer was probably to be repeated after each of the nine preceding petitions.

Chapter XV.

Hymn to Rā.

[From the Papyrus of Ani (Brit Mus. No. 10,470, sheet 20)]

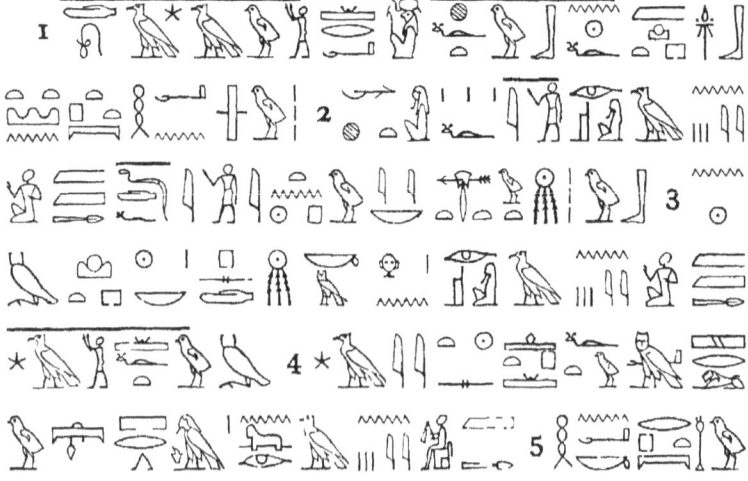

CHAP. XV] HYMN TO RĀ AT SUNRISE. 41

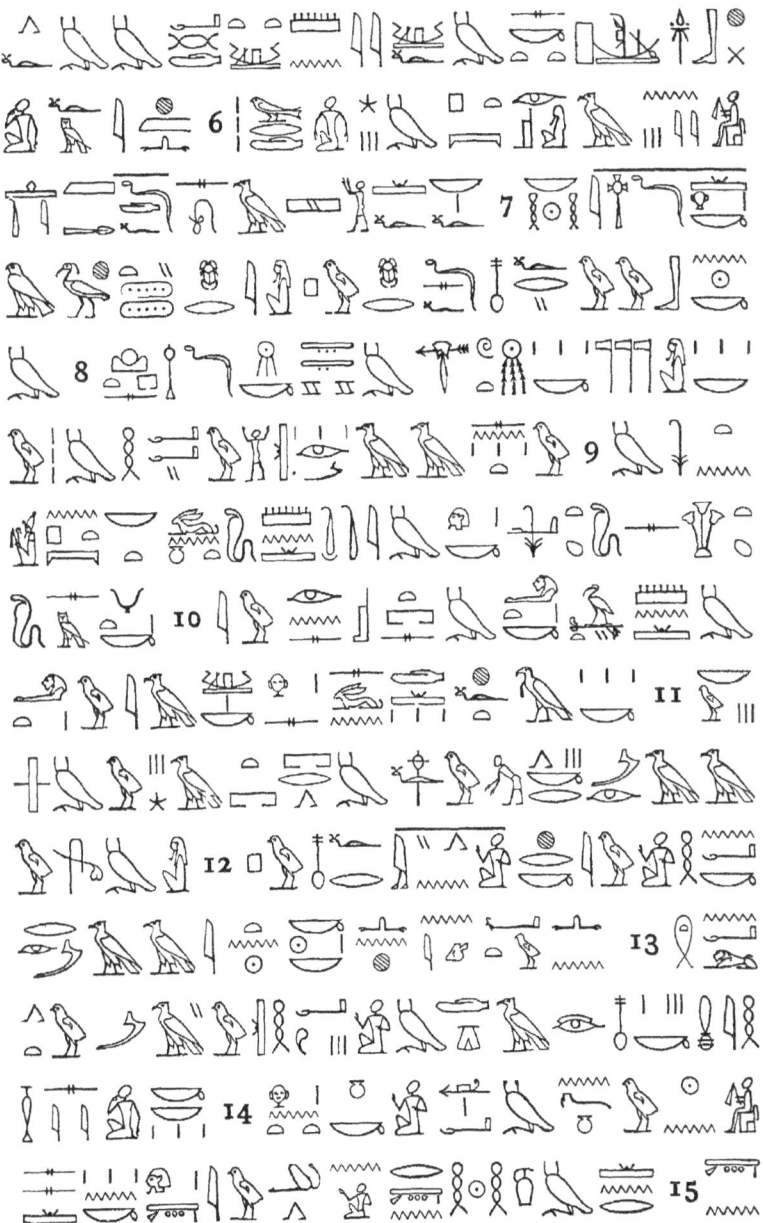

42 THE BOOK OF THE DEAD. [Chap. xv

CHAP. XV] HYMN TO RĀ AT SUNRISE. 43

CHAP. XV] HYMN TO RĀ AT SUNSET. 45

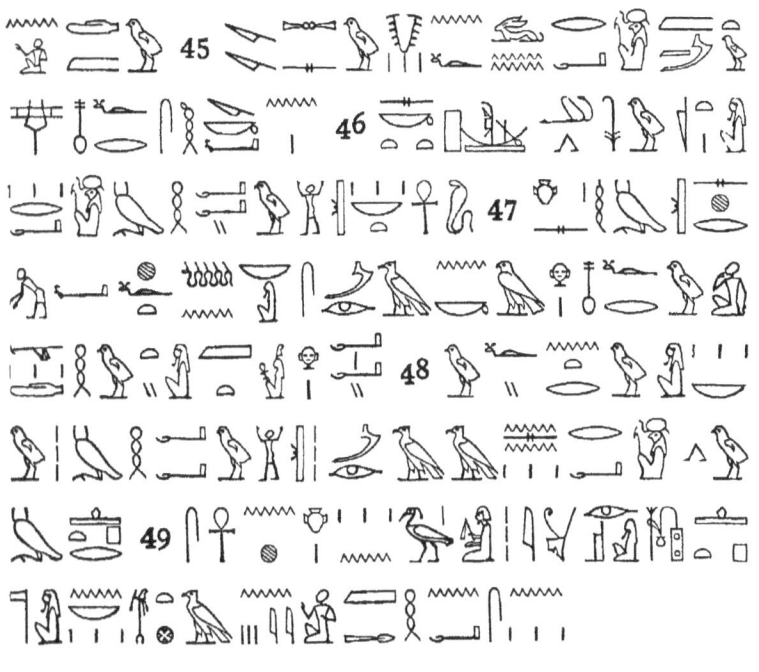

CHAPTER XV.

A Hymn to the setting Sun.

[From the Papyrus of Mut-ḥetep (Brit. Mus. No. 10,010, sheet 5).]

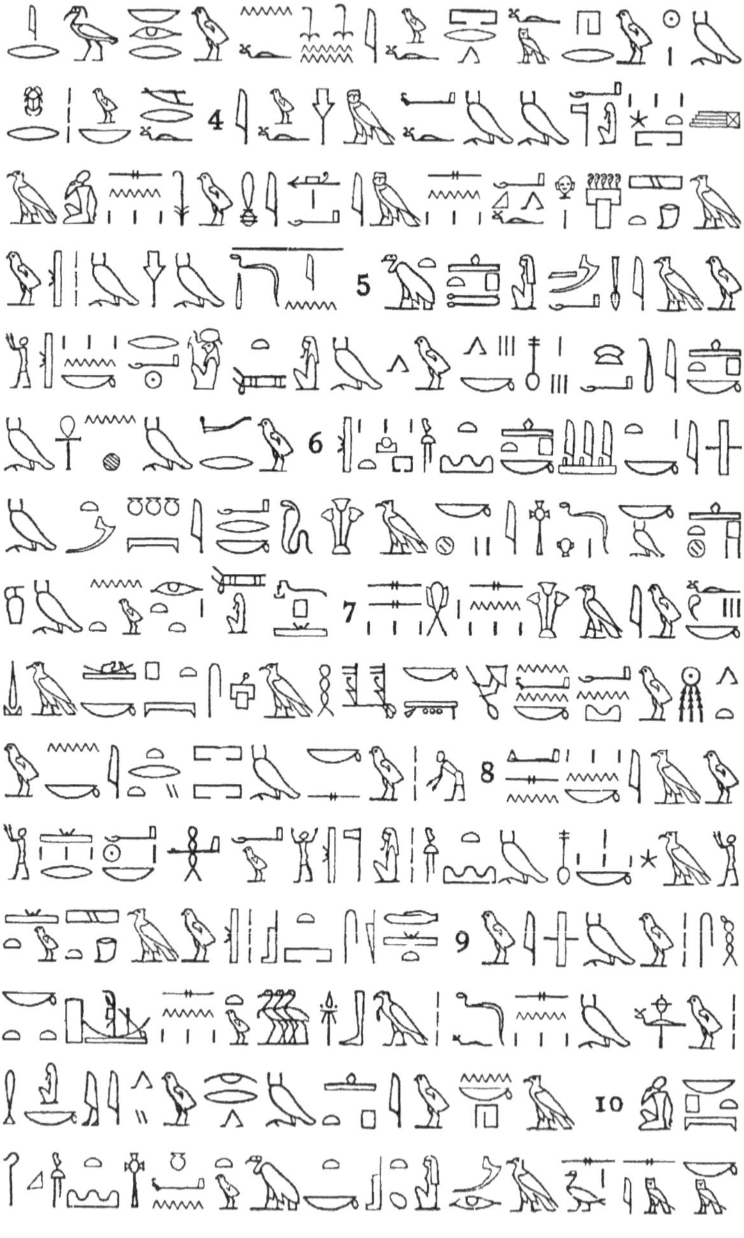

CHAP. XV] HYMN TO RĀ AT SUNSET. 47

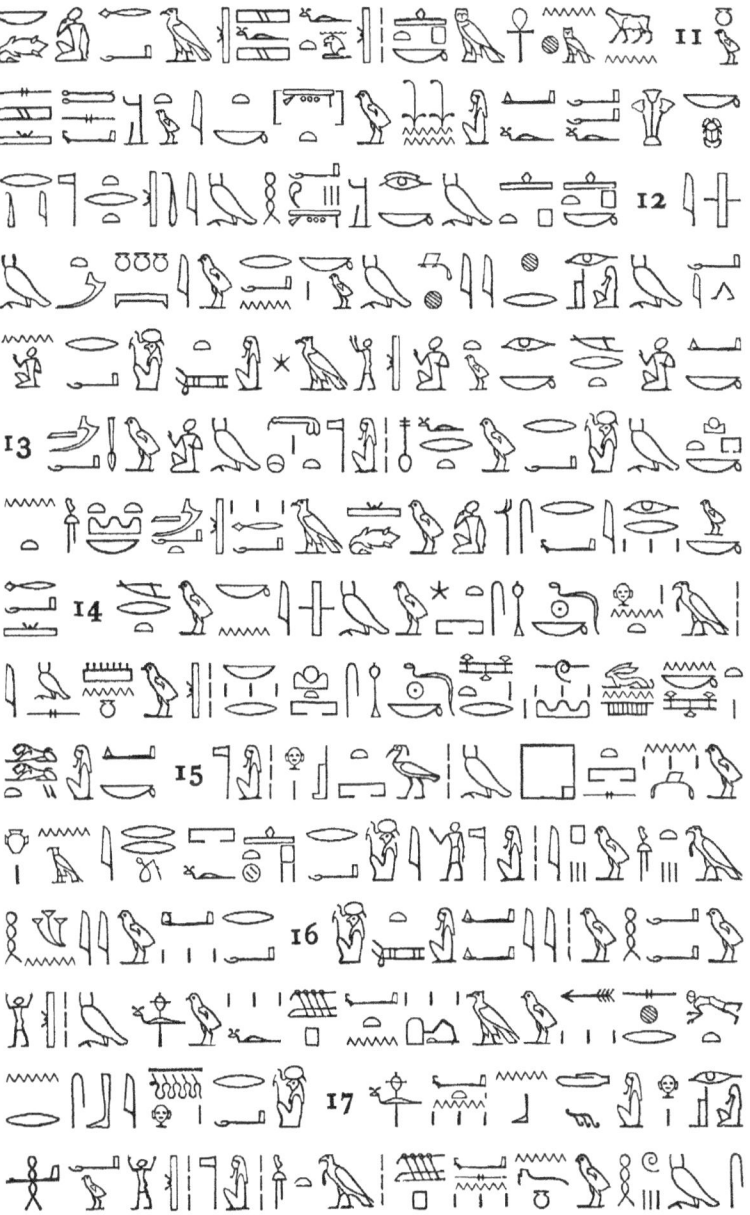

48   THE BOOK OF THE DEAD.   [Chap. xv

Chapter XV.
A Hymn to the setting Sun.
[From a Papyrus at Dublin (No. 4). See Naville, *Todtenbuch*, Bl. 19.]

HYMN TO RĀ.

50   VIGNETTE OF THE RISING SUN.   [CHAP. XVI

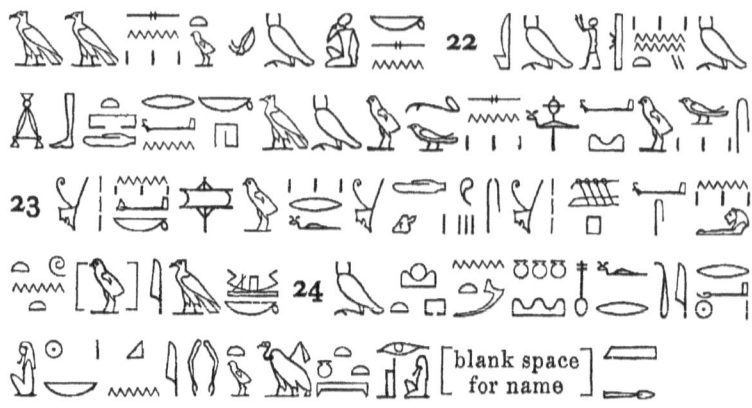

CHAPTER XVI.

The scene to which Lepsius inadvertently gave the number XVI and which he regarded as a Chapter of the Book of the Dead is, strictly speaking, only a Vignette intended to accompany the Hymn to Rā at Sunrise. In the Papyrus of Ani the Disk is seen supported by the hands of a pair of arms which proceed from the sign of "life", ☥; this, in its turn, is supported by the *tet*. Above is the vault of heaven, *i. e.*, the rounded end of the Ṭuat, and on each side of the Disk are three apes, or spirits of the dawn, with their paws raised in adoration. On one side of the kneels Nephthys, and on the other Isis; beneath each goddess is the sign for

CHAP. XVI] VIGNETTE OF THE SETTING SUN. 51

"gold" ⌢, and both they and the 𓋹 rest on the horizon ⌣. Some papyri have a Vignette accompanying the Hymn to Rā at Sunset. In the Papyrus of Qenna Rā appears in the form of a hawk resting on a standard, with the solar Disk on his head 𓅃. Before him kneel three hawk-headed gods,[1] each having his left arm raised, and behind him kneel three jackal-headed gods,[2] each having his right arm raised. Below this scene is a smaller one, in the centre of which we see a cluster of lotus plants and two seated lions, each with a disk on his head. On one side kneels Isis, and on the other Nephthys, each goddess having her hands raised in adoration of the Lion-gods, one of whom symbolizes the rising sun and the other the setting sun. In a papyrus at Dublin the setting sun appears on the standard of Āmentet 𓋀, which rests on the horizon, with bread and ale 𓎬, and the god is adored by four ape-gods and two gods and two goddesses.

1. Their names are Horus, Mesthà and Ḥāpi.
2. Their names are Horus, Ṭuamutef and Qebḥsennuf.

Chapter XVII.

[From the Papyrus of Iuâu (Davis Papyrus, ed. Naville, plate 12)]

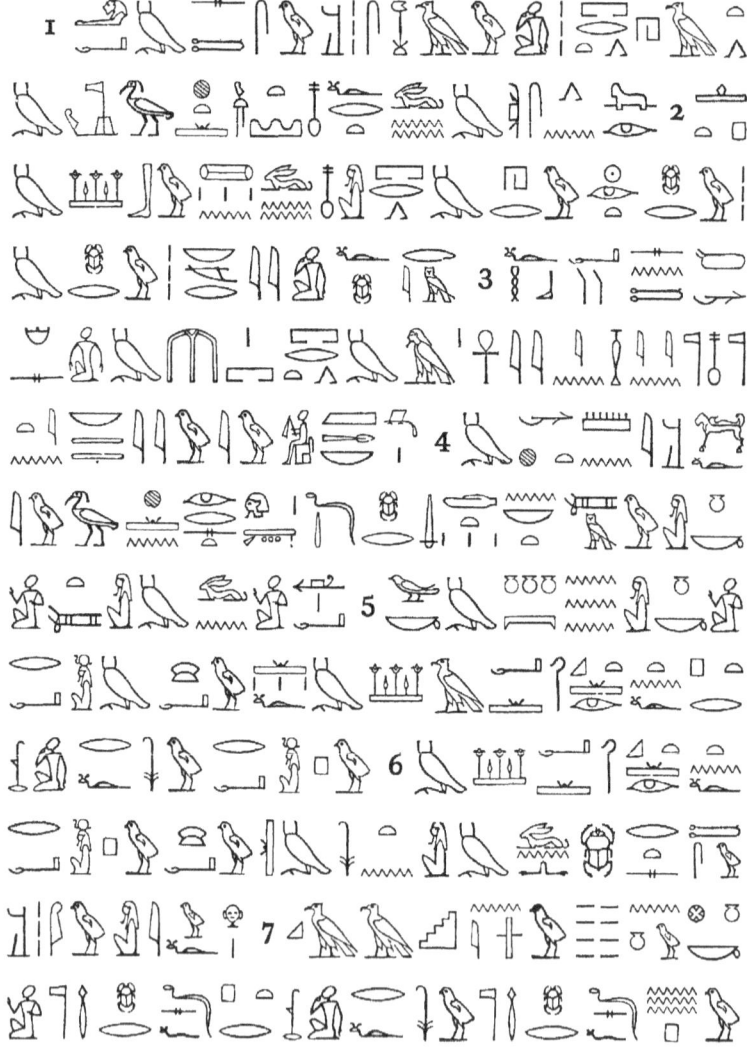

CHAPTER XVII.

[From the Papyrus of Nebseni (Brit. Mus. No. 9,900, sheet 13).]

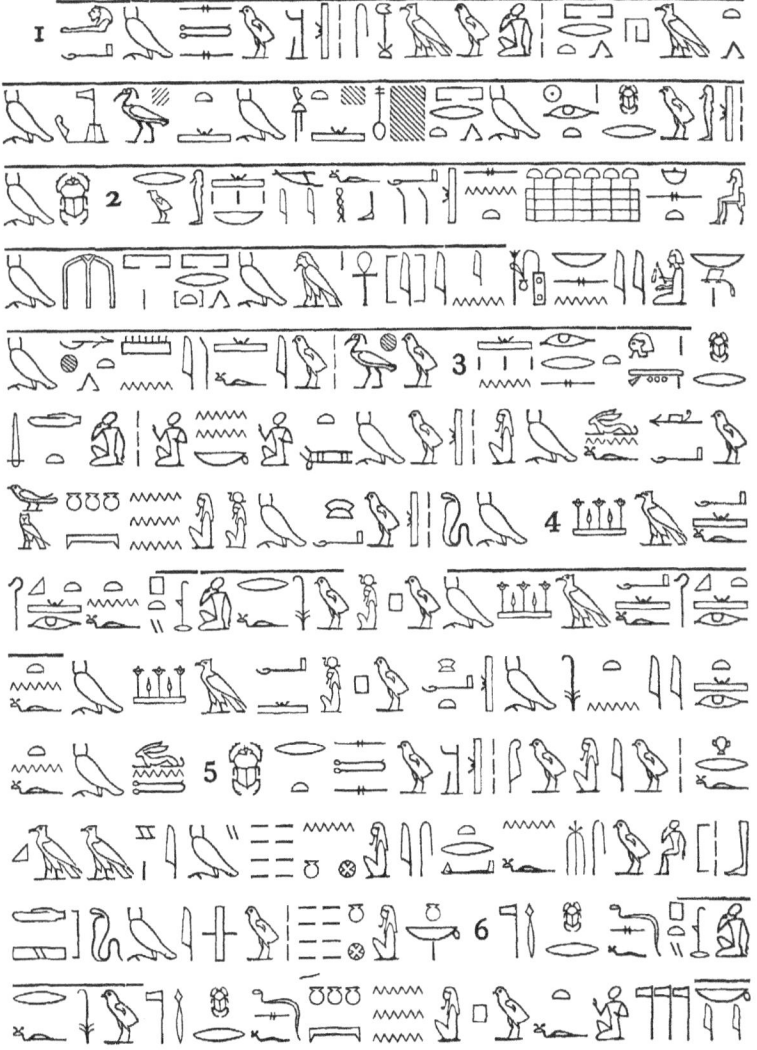

54 RĀ AND HIS NAMES. [Chap. XVII

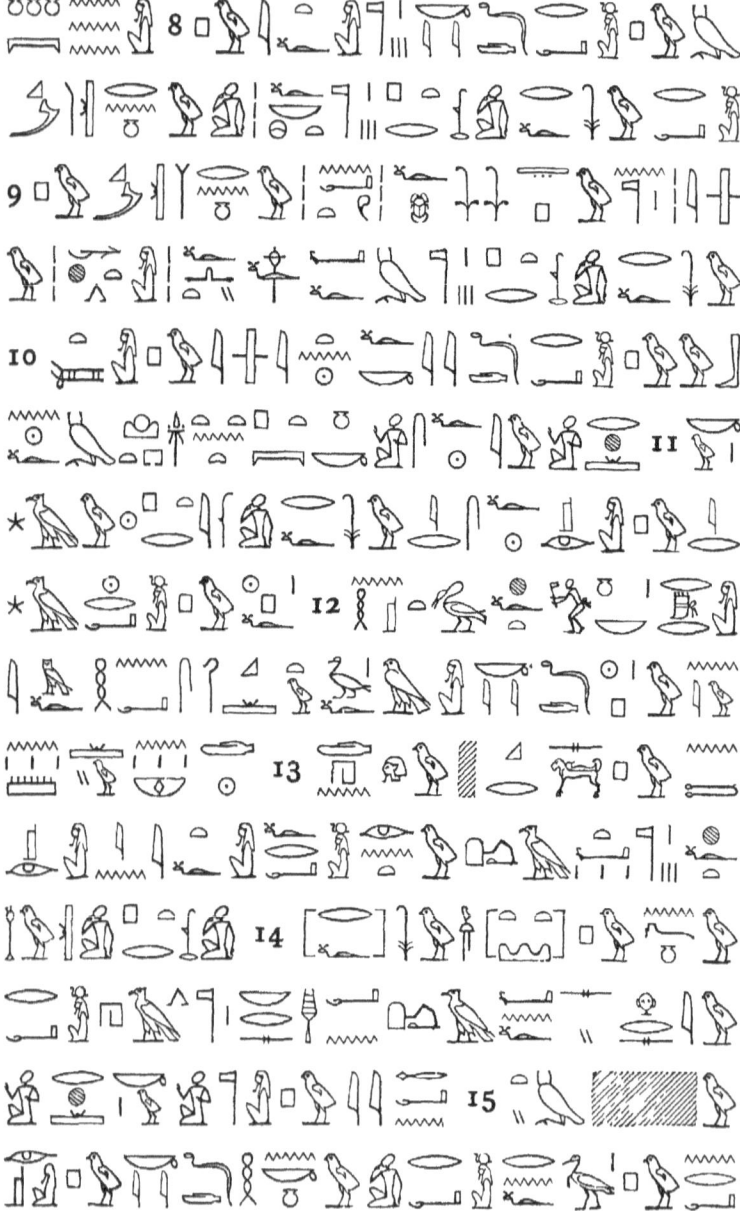

RĀ AND HIS NAMES.

THE DOOR OF THE TUAT. [Chap. XVII

CHAP. XVII] THE DOOR OF THE TUAT. 59

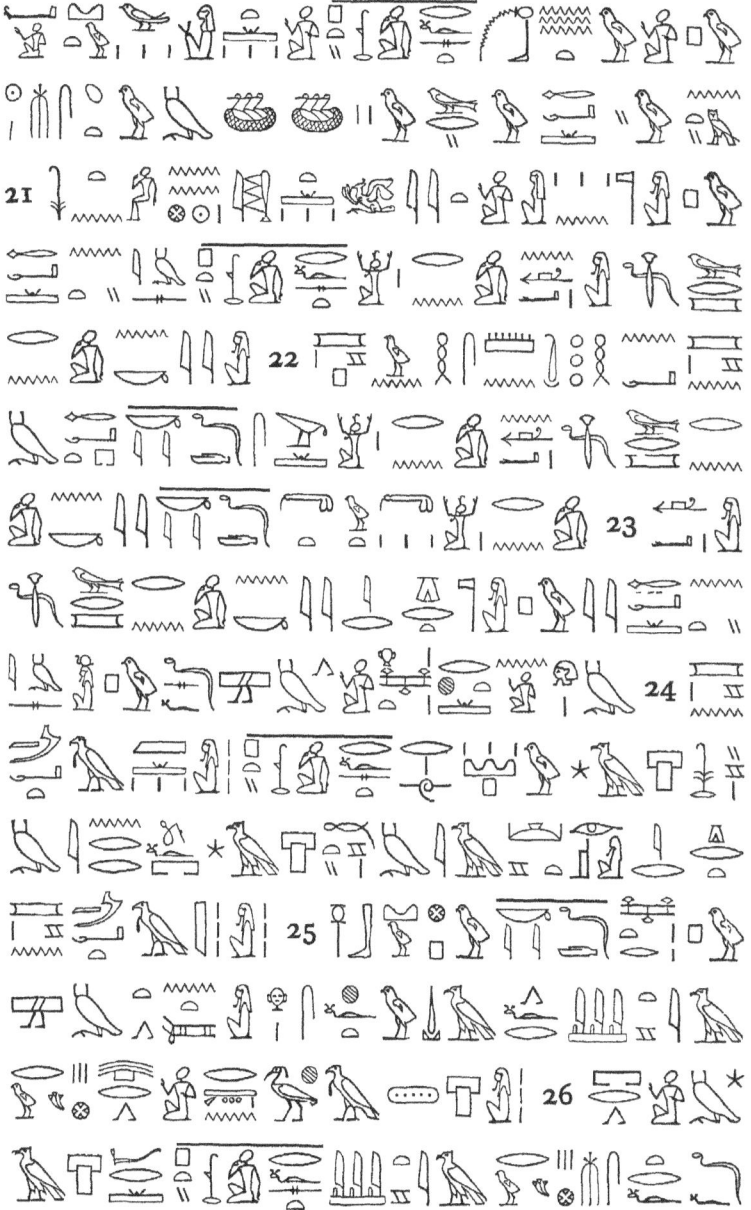

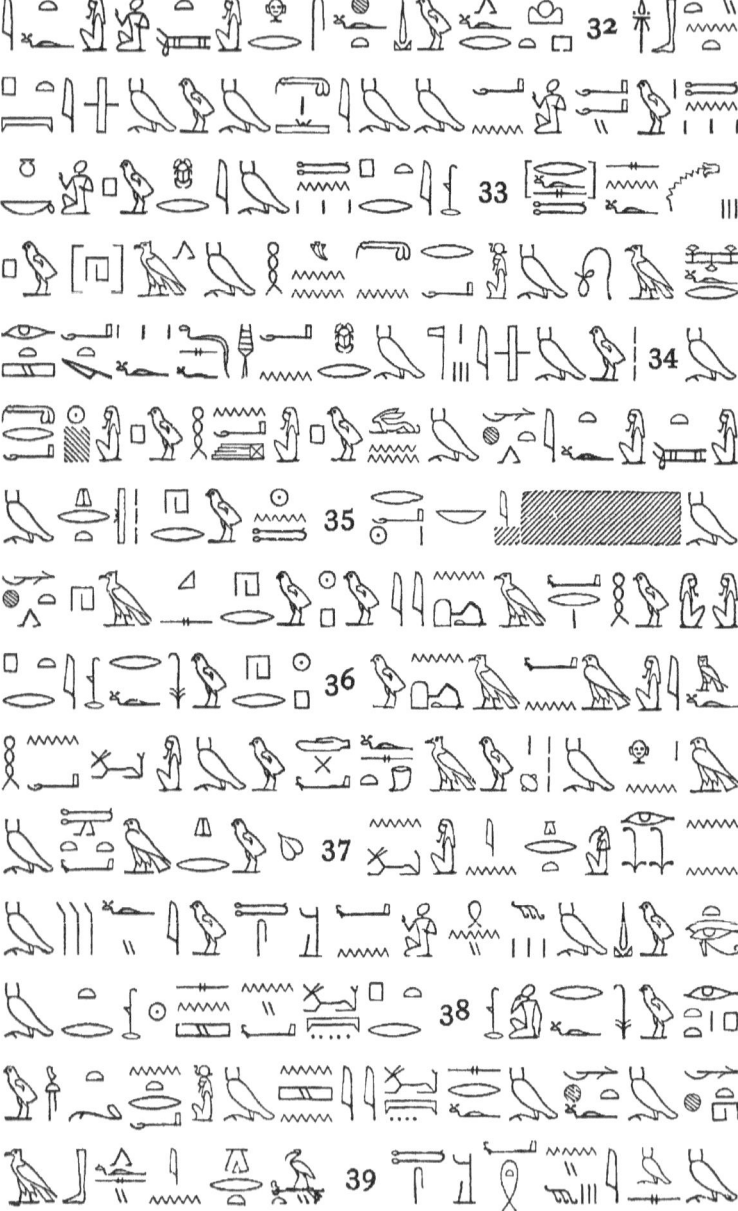

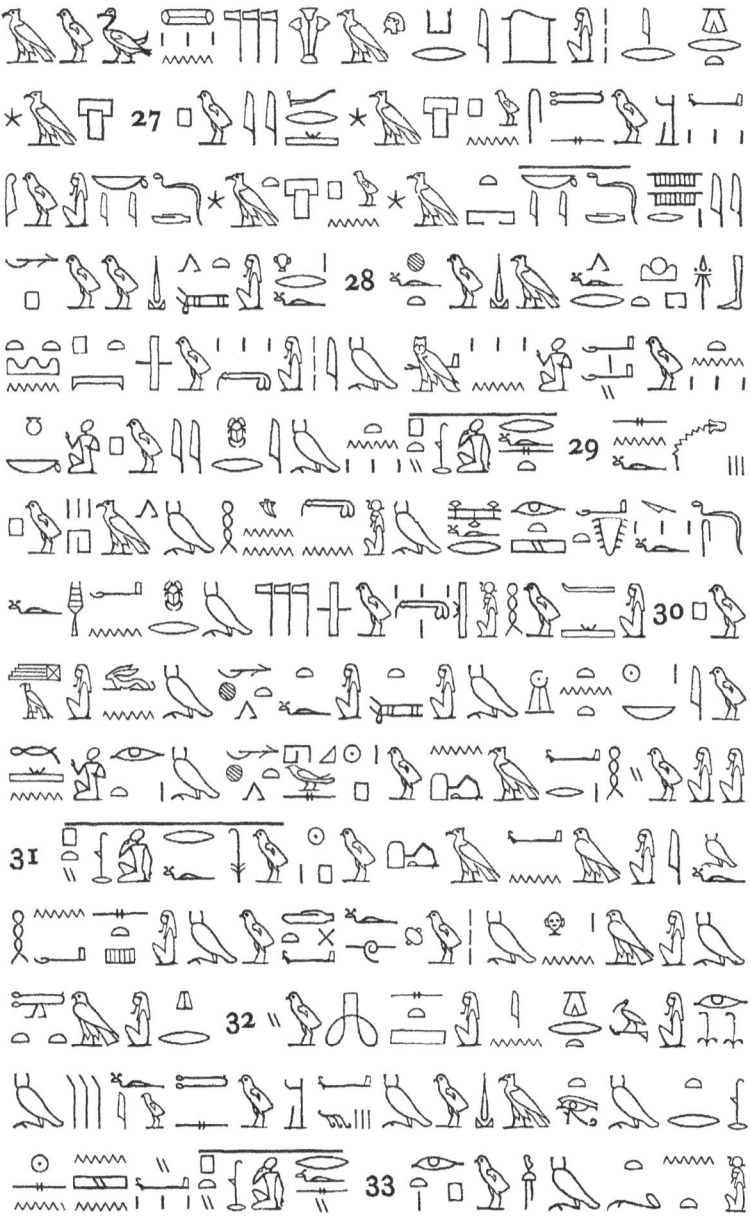

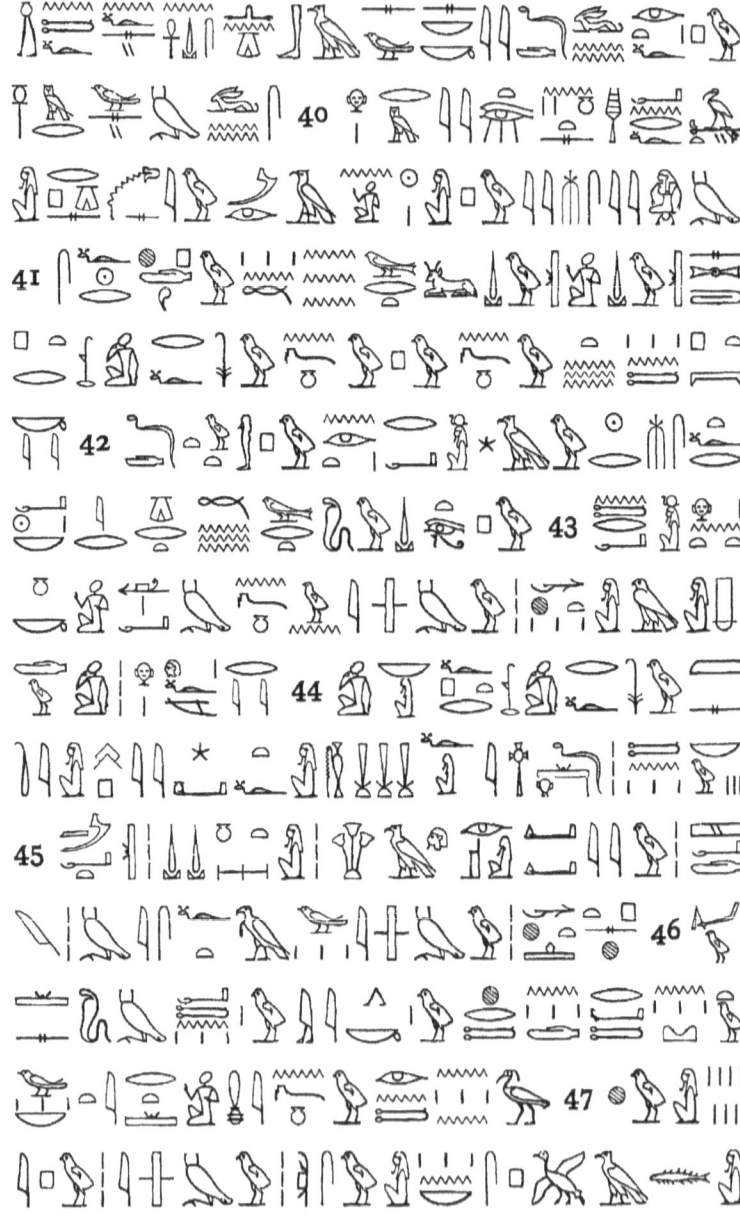

THE COW MEḤURIT.

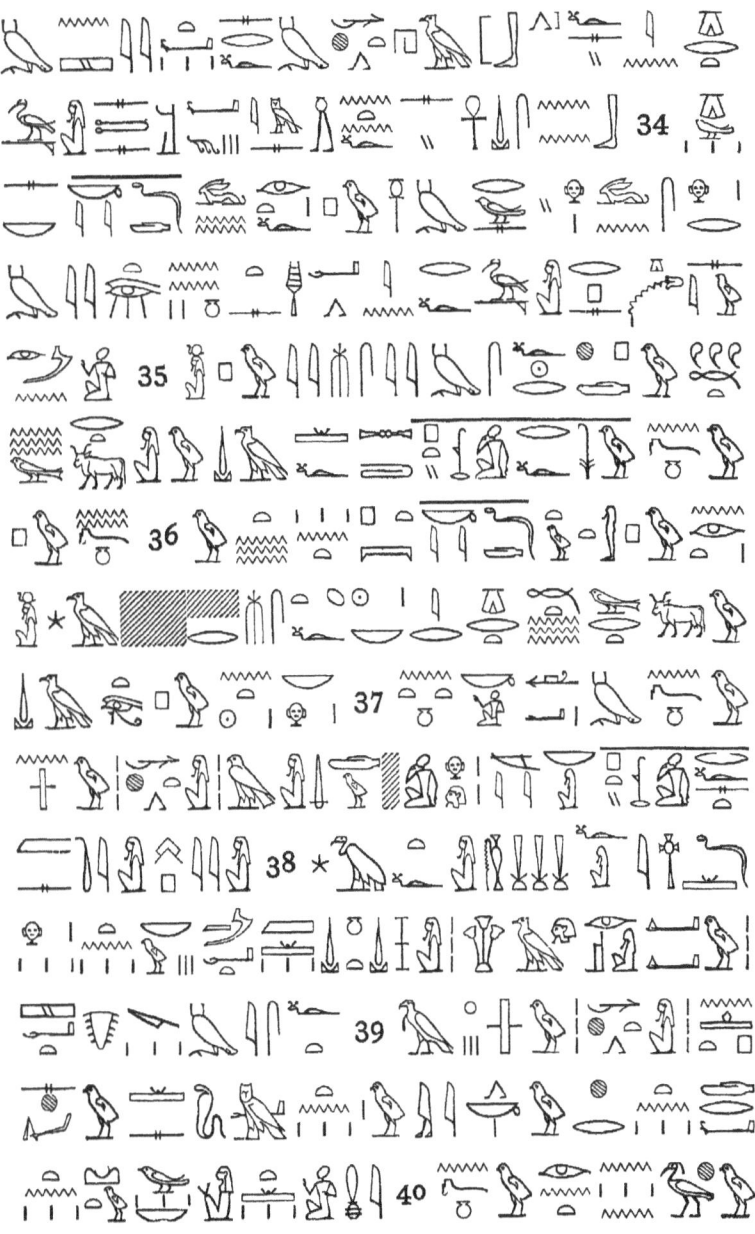

64 THE SEVEN SPIRITS. [CHAP. XVII

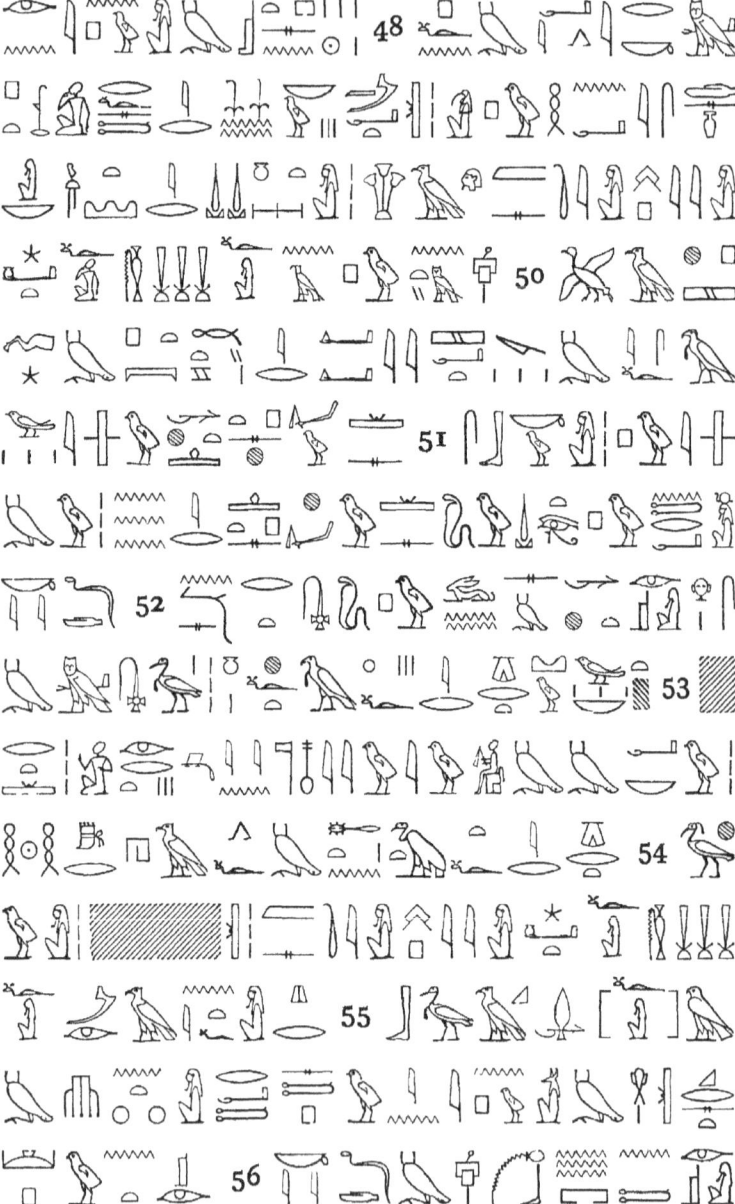

CHAP. XVII] SEPA AND ḤETEP-SEKHUS.

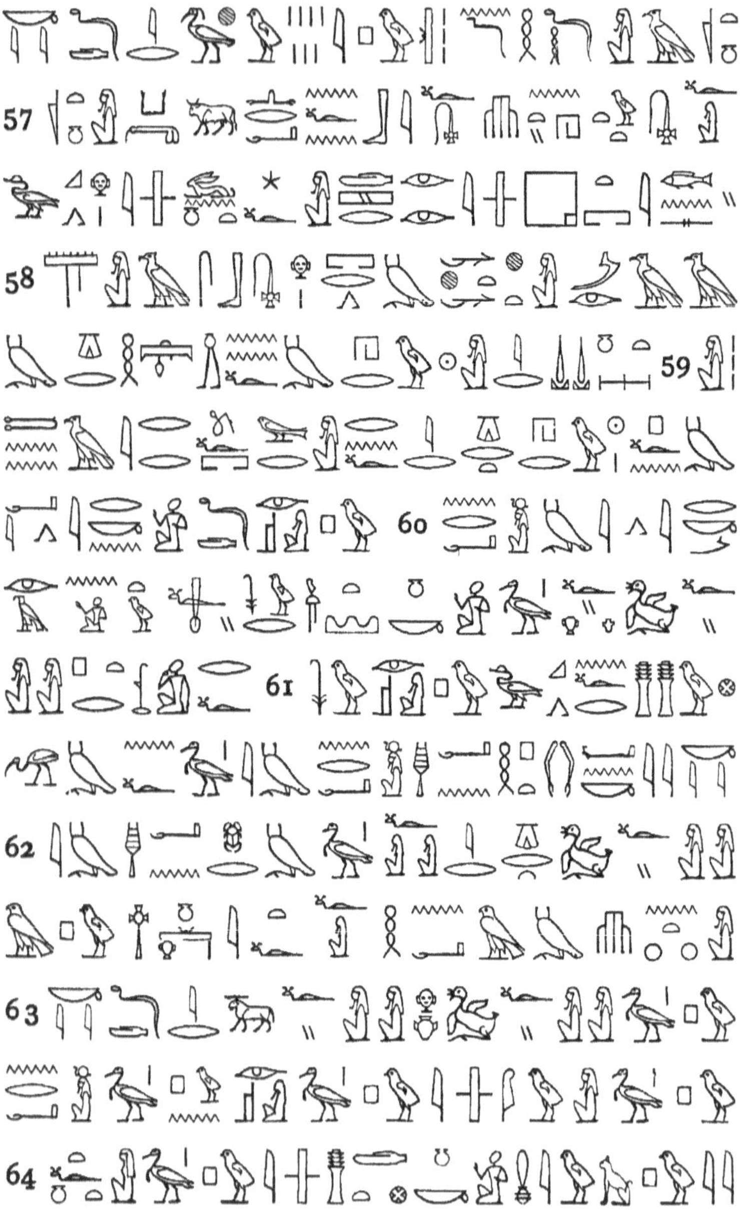

CHAP. XVII] THE DOUBLE SOUL IN THE TCHAFUI.

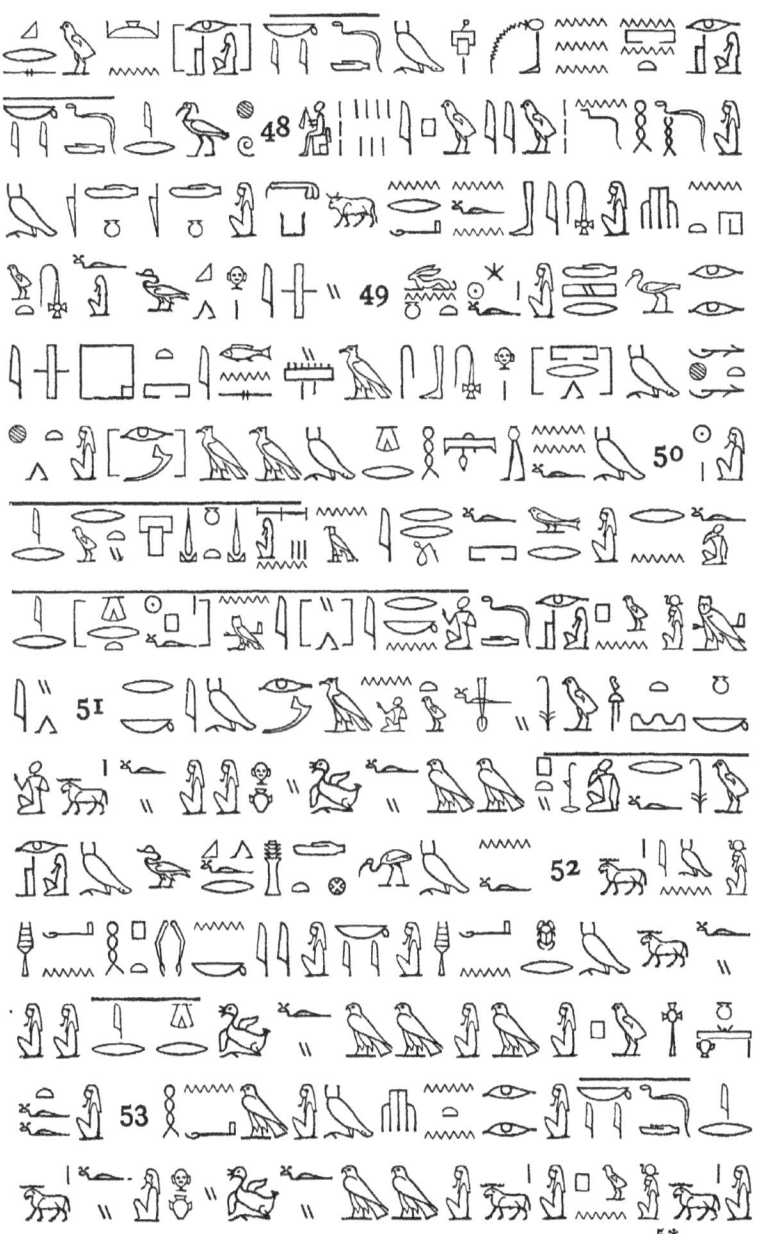

CHAP. XVII] THE CAT BY THE PERSEA TREE. 69

70 THE BOOK OF THE DEAD. [Chap. XVII

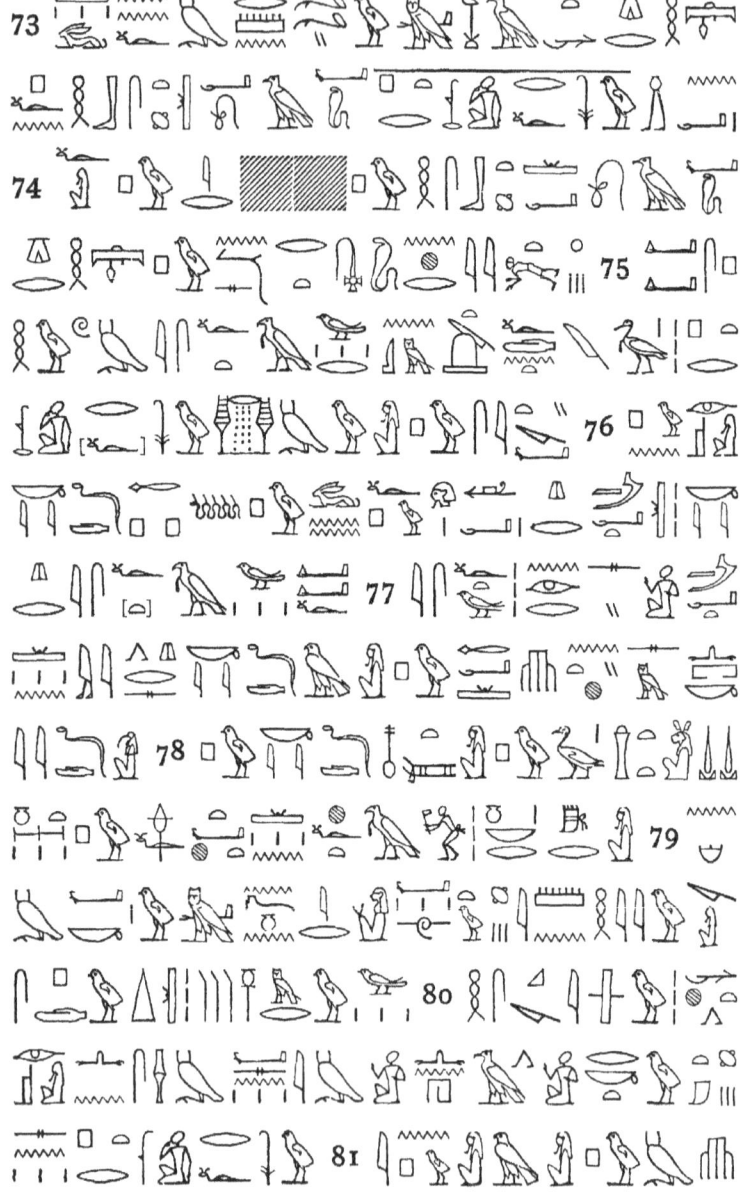

THE EXECUTIONER OF OSIRIS.

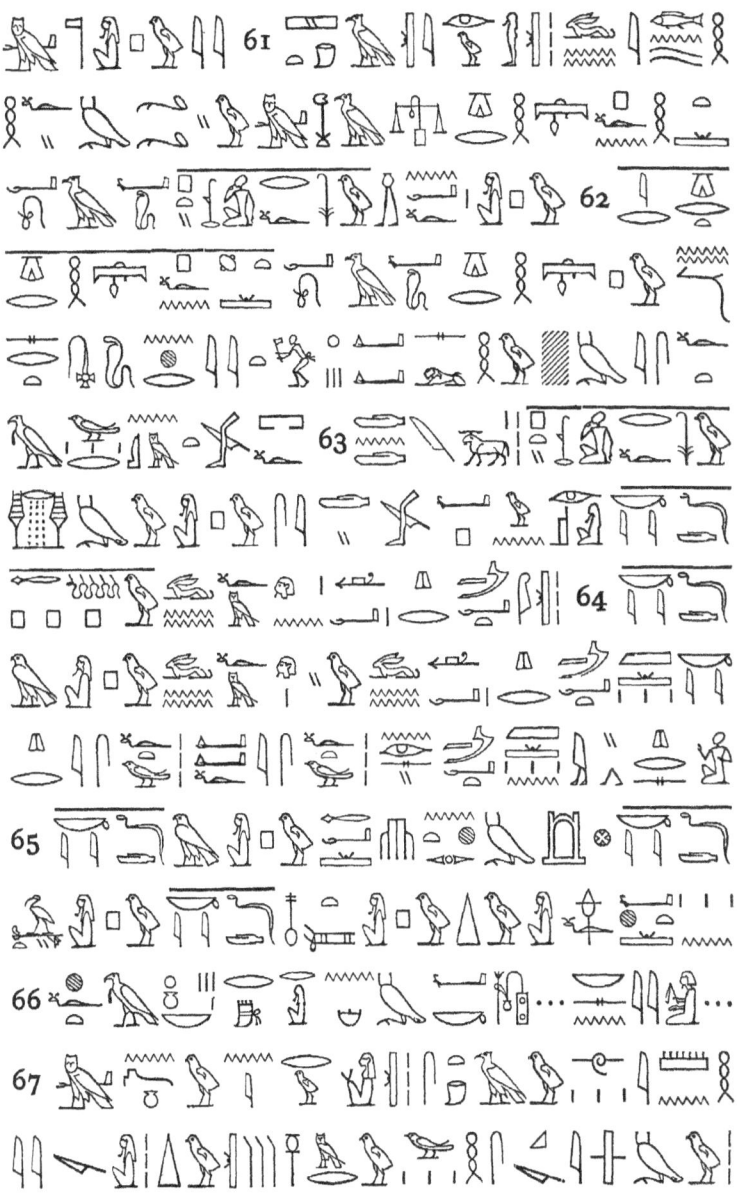

72 THE BOOK OF THE DEAD. [Chap. XVII

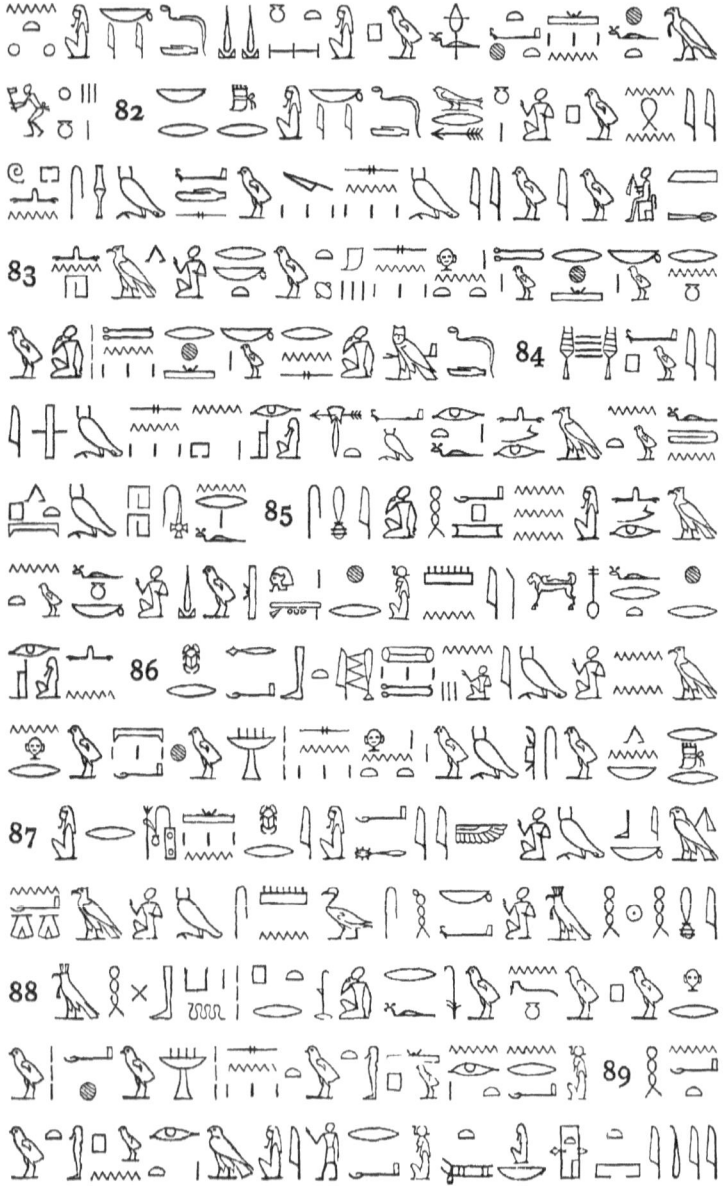

THE GOD NEḤEB-KAU.

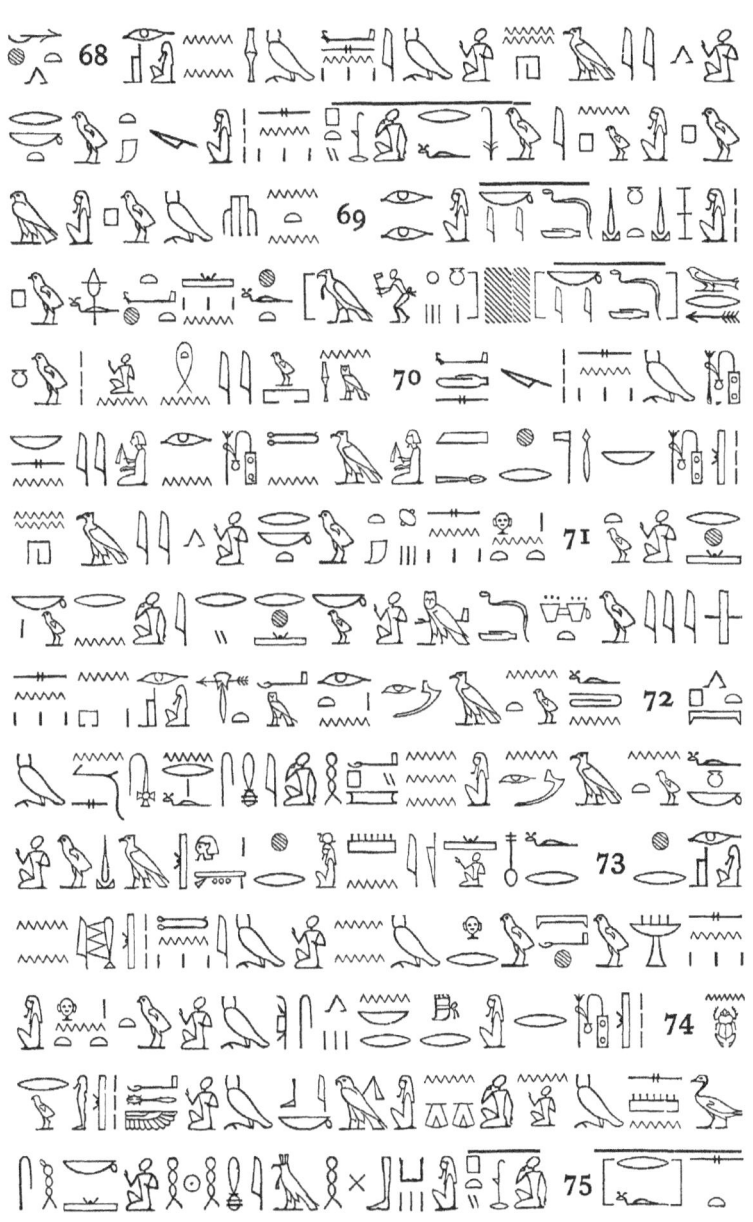

74 THE BOOK OF THE DEAD. [Chap. xvii

THE DOG-FACED GOD.

76 THE BOOK OF THE DEAD. [Chap. XVII

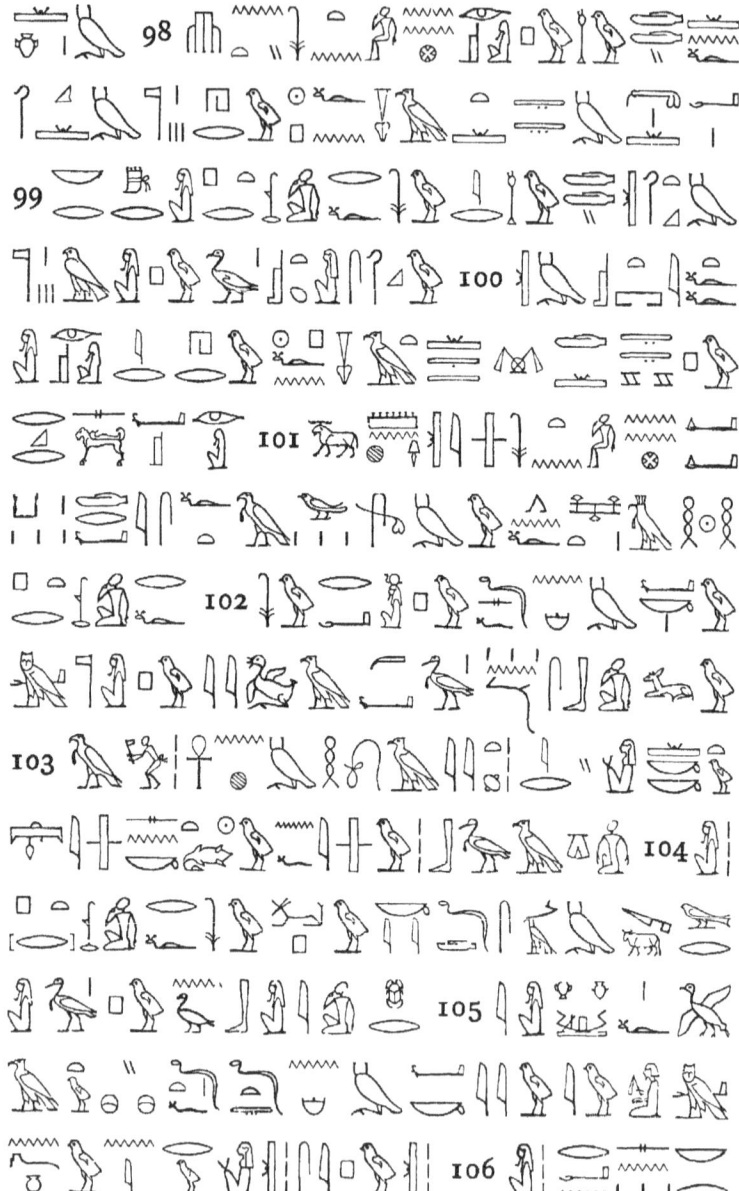

OSIRIS AND HIS CROWN.

78 THE BOOK OF THE DEAD. [Chap. XVII

THE MESQET.

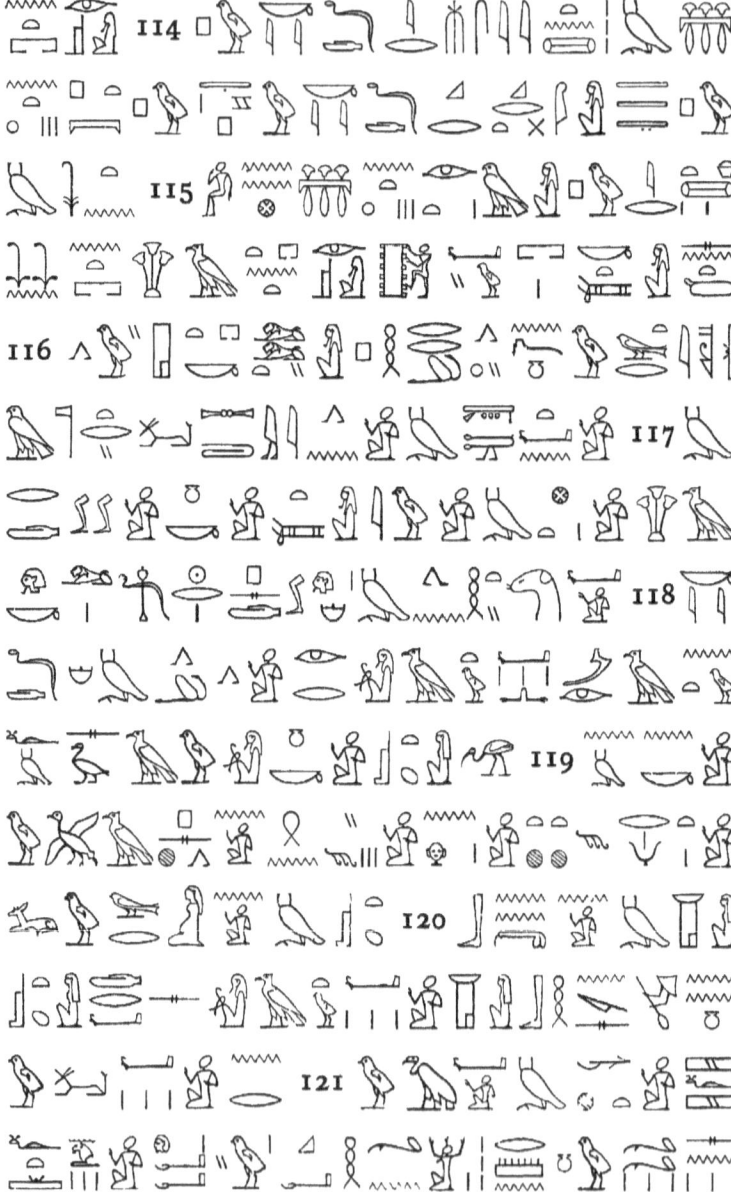

CHAP. XVII] THE EYE OF HORUS. 81

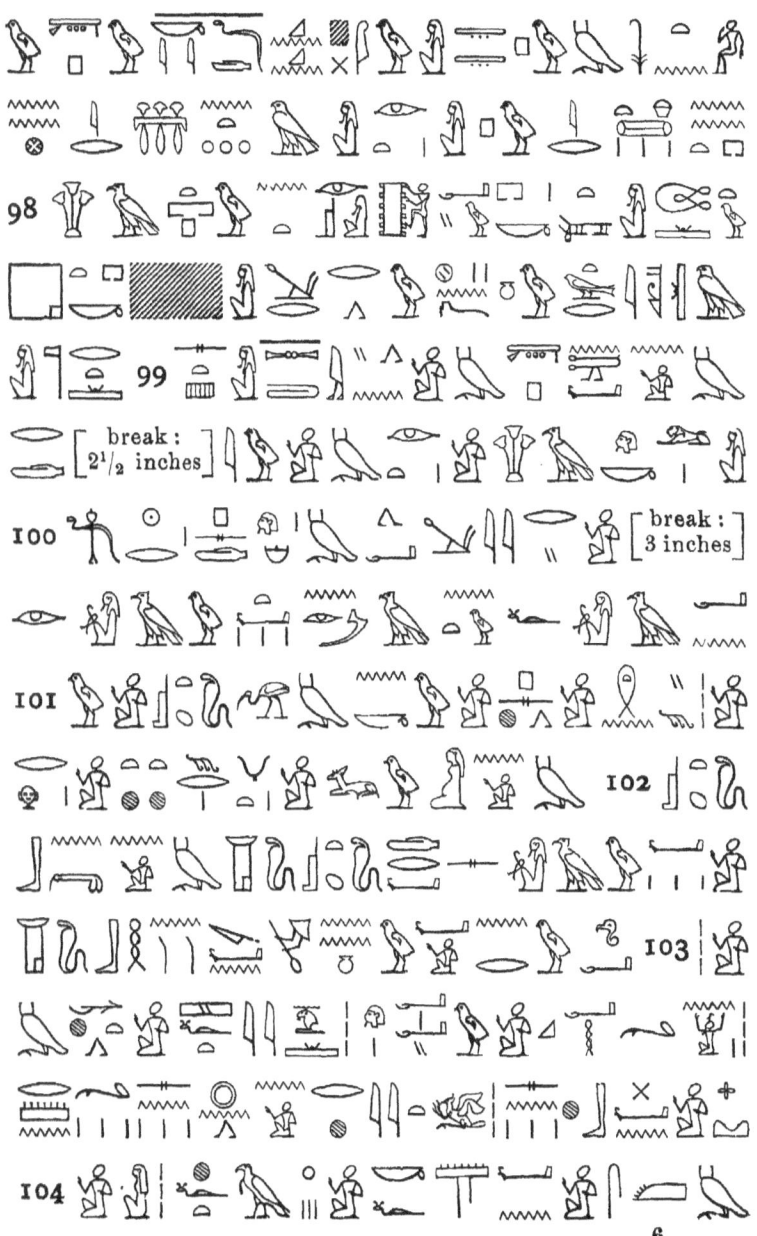

82 THE BOOK OF THE DEAD. [Chap. XVII

THE PHALLUS OF OSIRIS.

Chapter XVII.

[From the Papyrus of Ani (Brit. Mus. No. 10,470, sheets 7—10).]

CHAP. XVII] YESTERDAY AND TO-DAY. 85

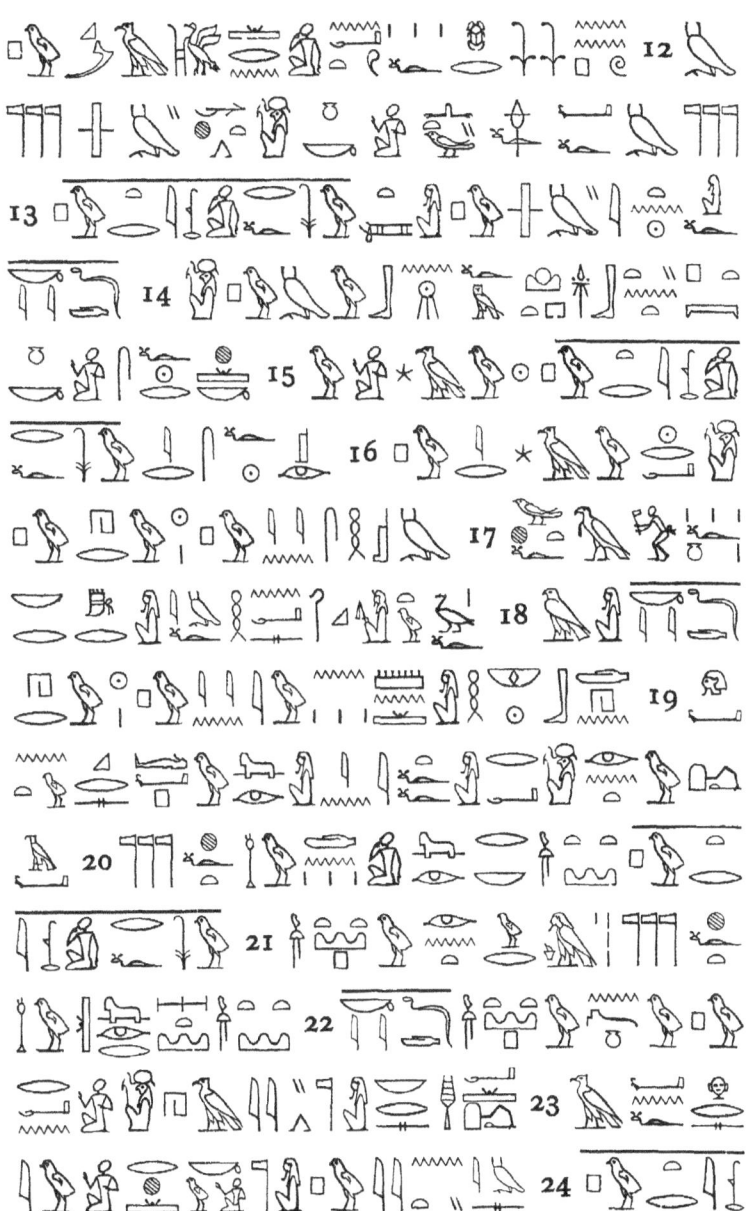

86 THE BOOK OF THE DEAD. [Chap. XVII

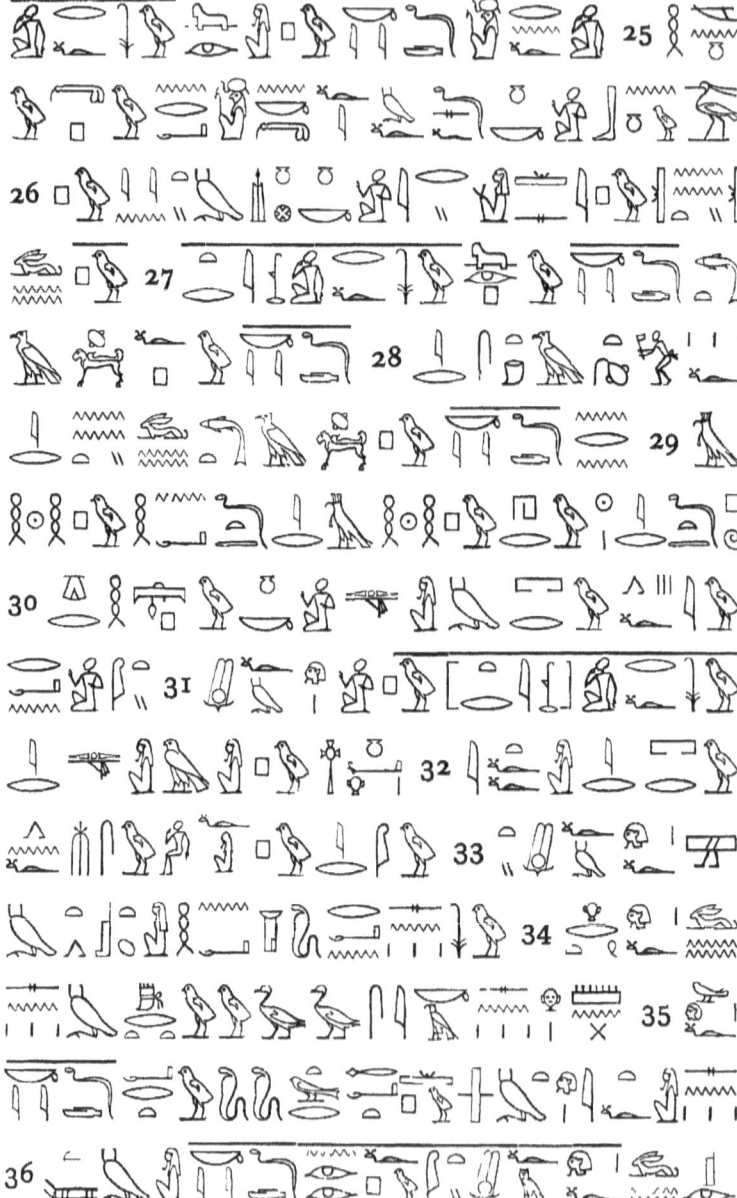

CHAP. XVII] THE TWO LAKES. 87

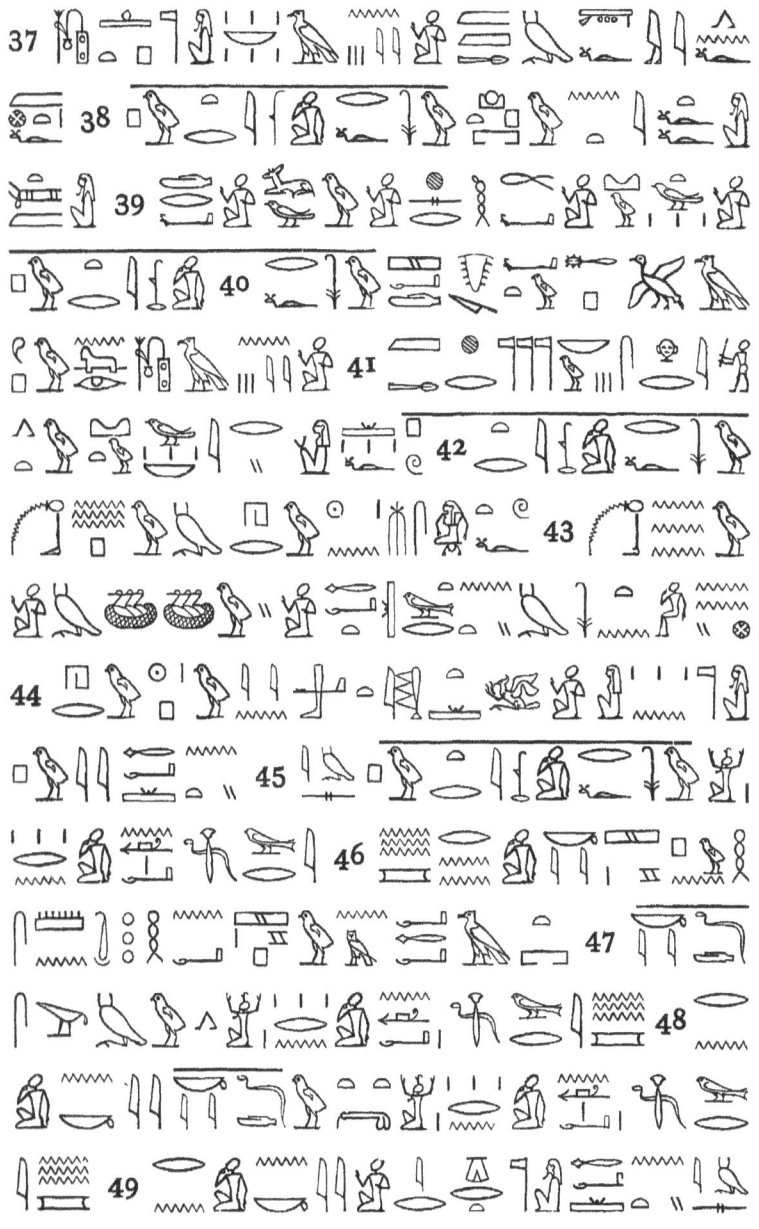

88 THE BOOK OF THE DEAD. [Chap. xvii

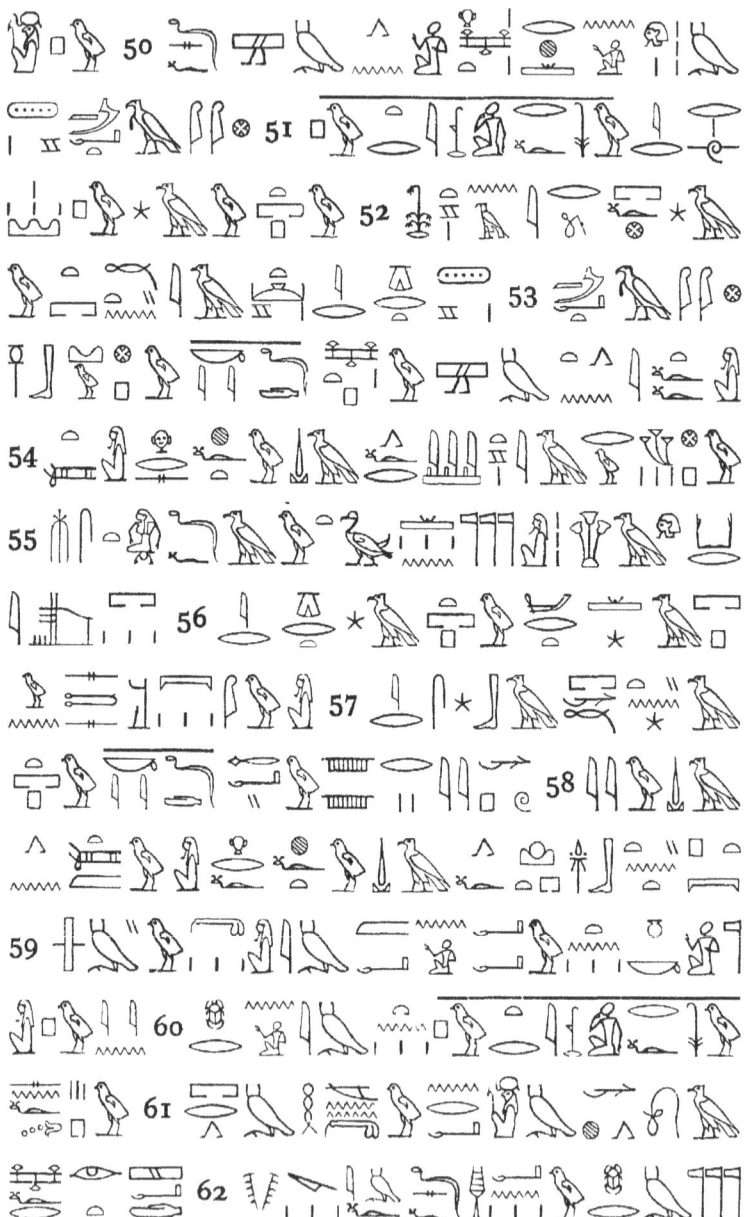

CHAP. XVII] THE TWO COMBATANT GODS

90 THE BOOK OF THE DEAD. [Chap. XVII

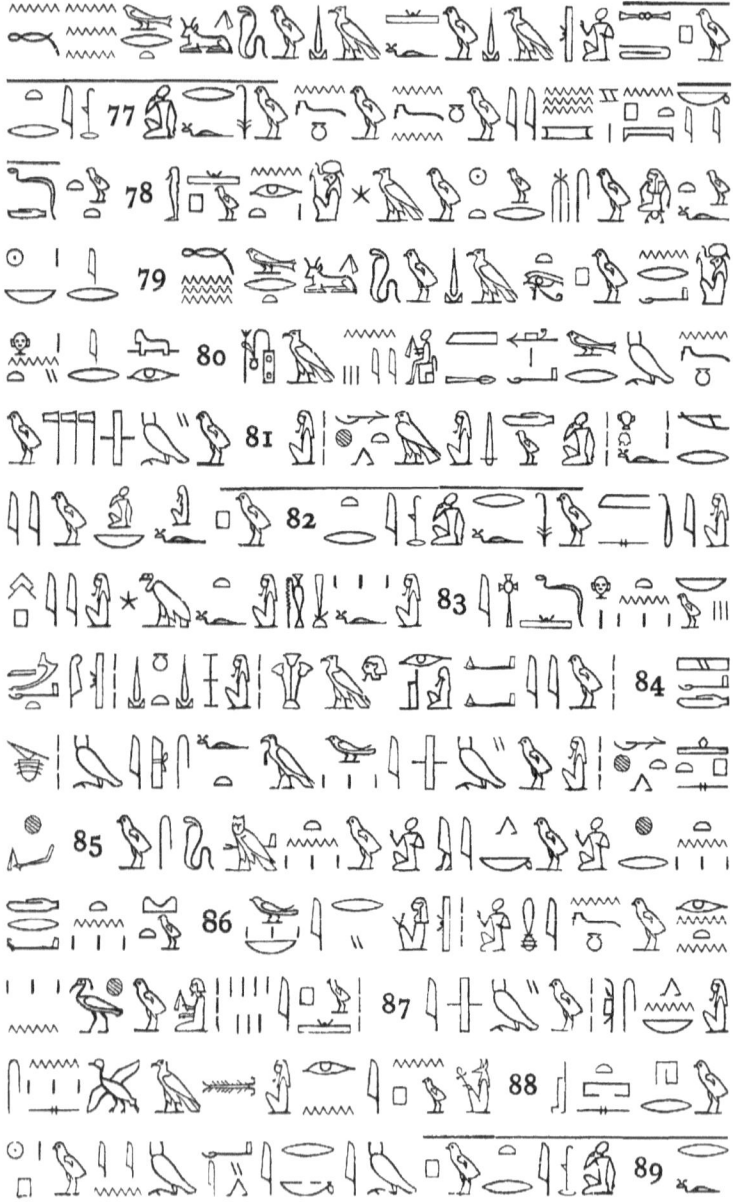

CHAP. XVII] THE SEVEN SPIRITS. 91

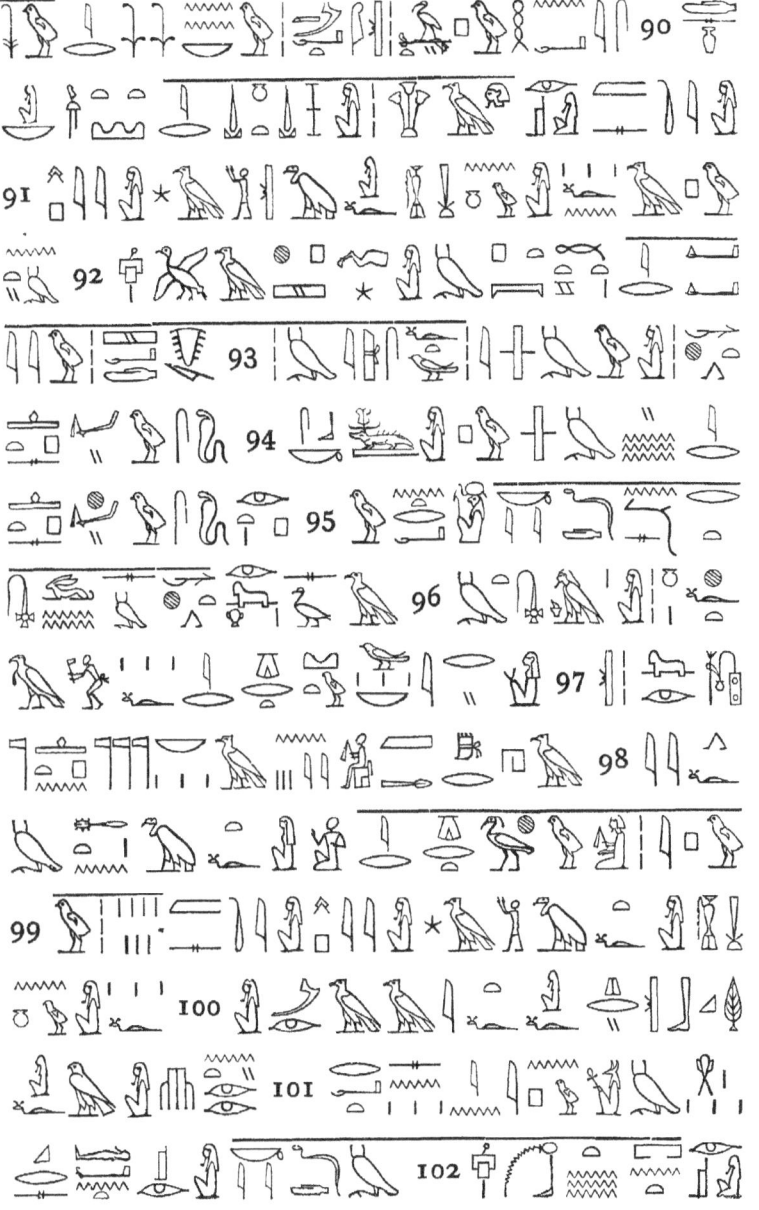

92 THE BOOK OF THE DEAD. [Chap. XVII

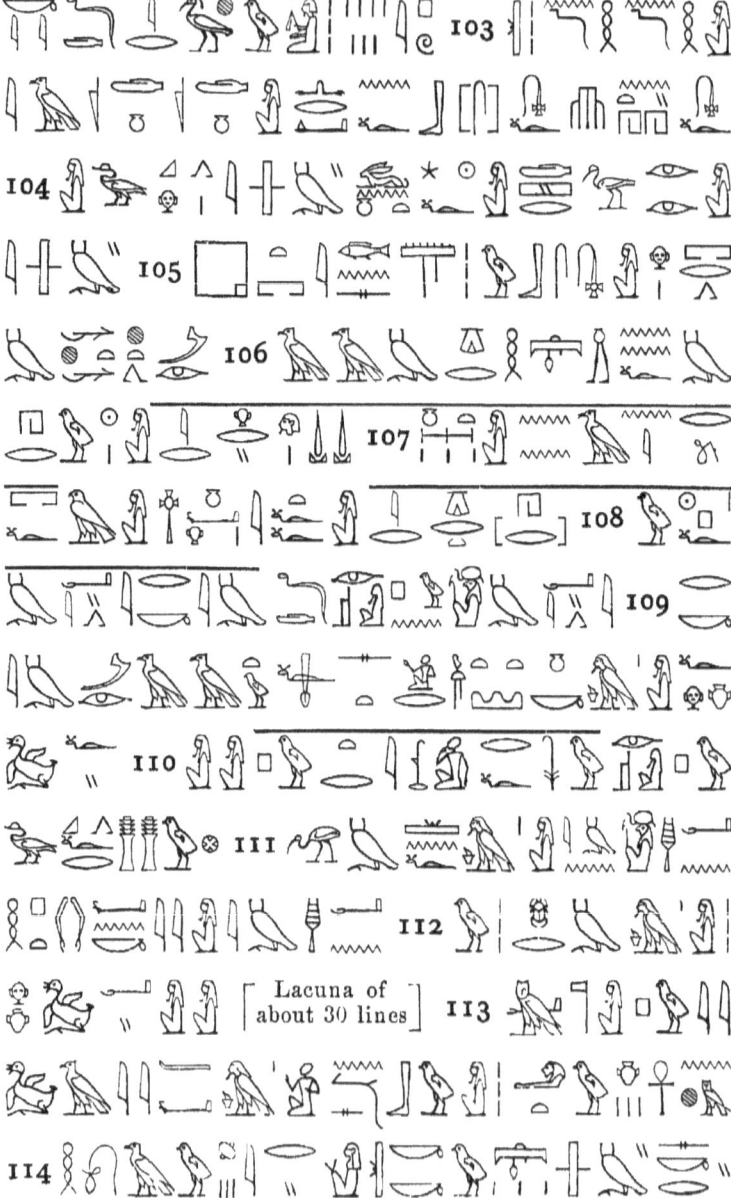

CHAP. XVII]   THE ASSESSORS.   93

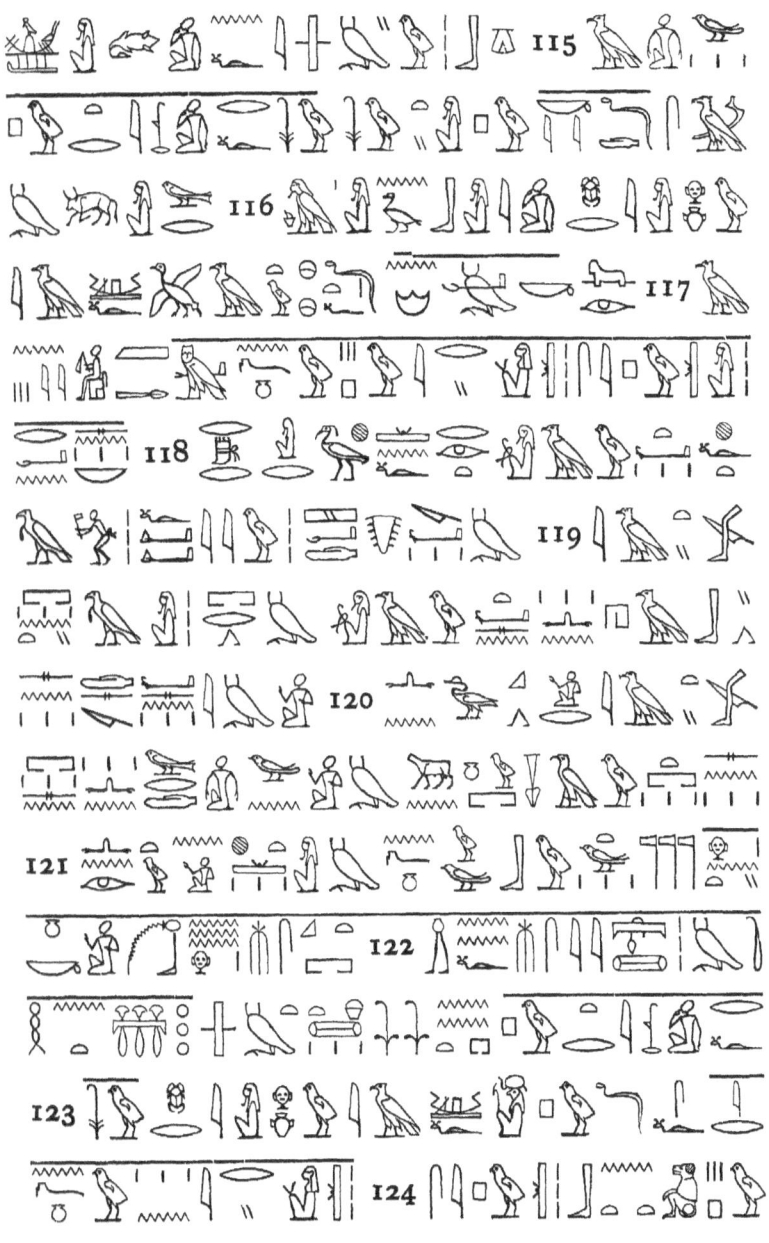

THE BOOK OF THE DEAD. [Chap. XVII

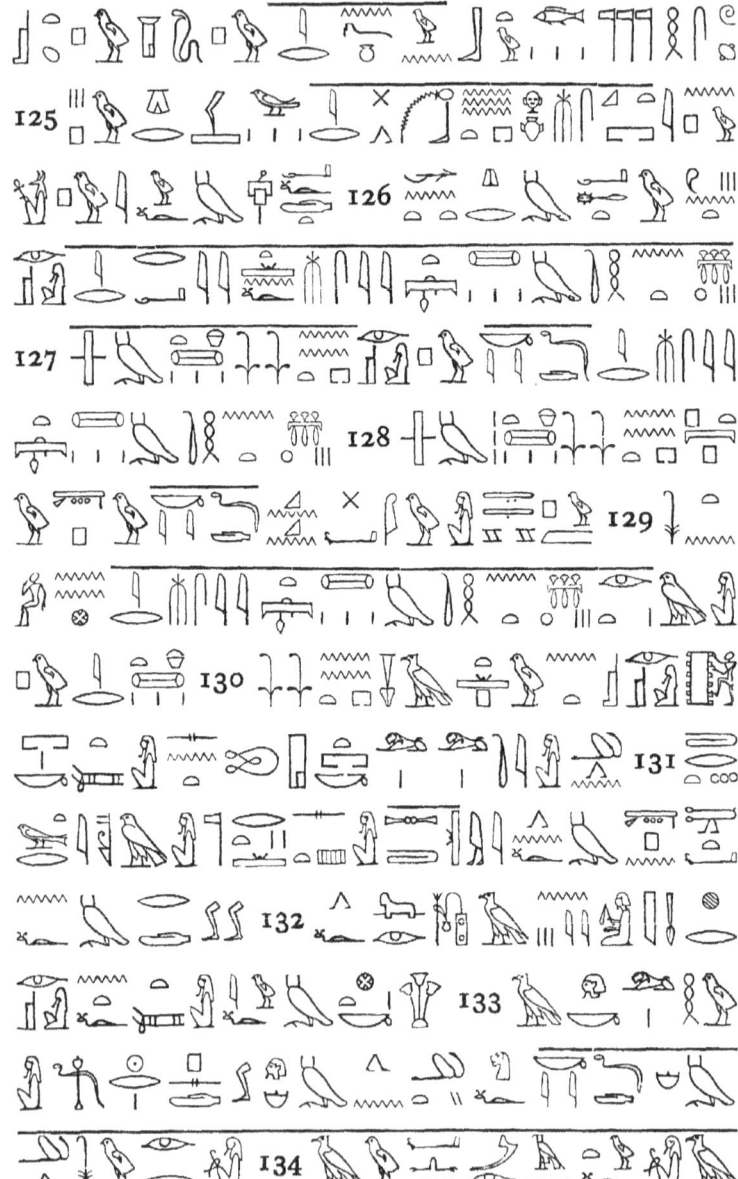

CHAP. XVII] THE PHALLUS OF OSIRIS 95

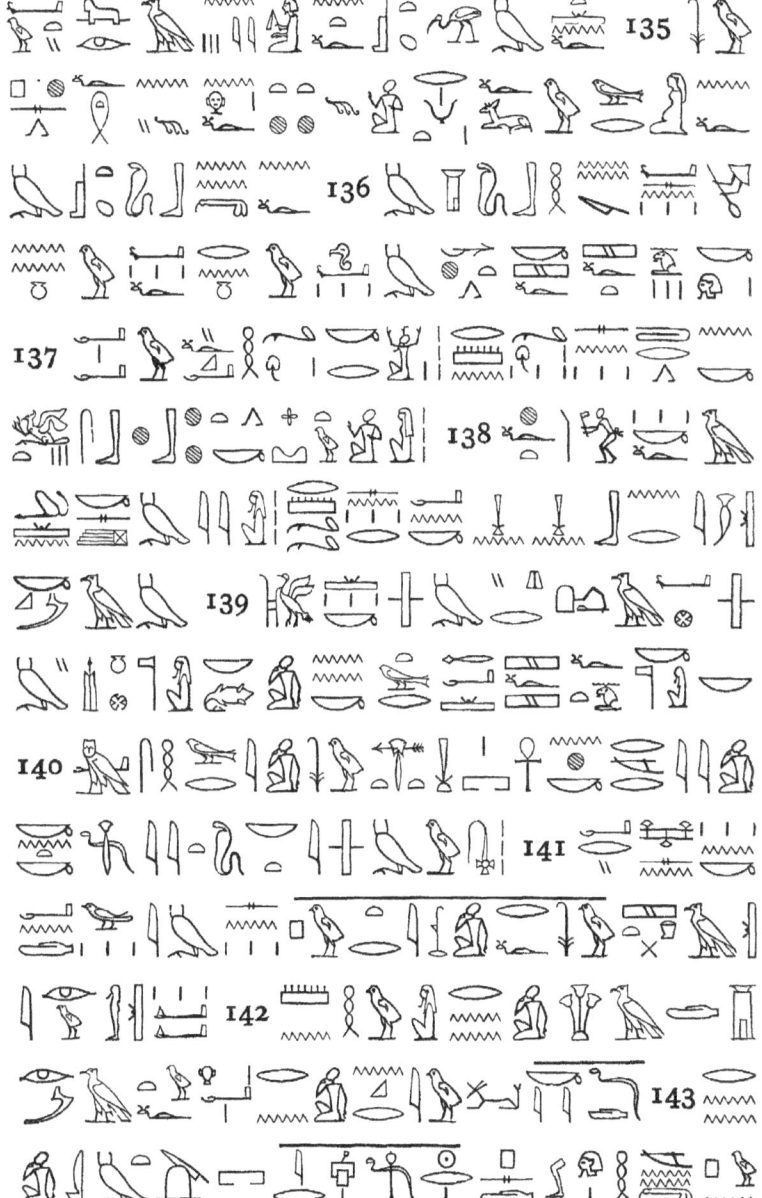

Chapter XVIII.

Introduction.

[From the Papyrus of Ani (Brit. Mus. No. 10,470, sheet 12).]

CHAP. XVIII]   LITANY TO THOTH.   97

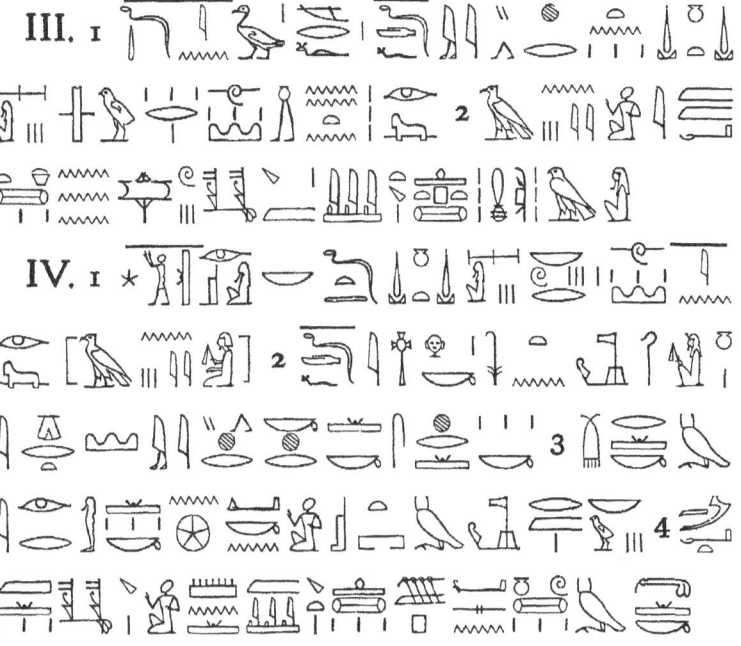

CHAPTER XVIII.

[A. From the Papyrus of Nebseni (Brit. Mus. No. 9,900, sheet 15) and from the Papyrus of Ani (Brit. Mus. No. 10,470, sheets 13 and 14)]
[B. From the Coffin of Paneḥem-Àst (ed. Bergmann, *Jahrbuch*, II, 1, 2. Vienna, 1883).]

98 THE BOOK OF THE DEAD. [Chap. XVIII

CHAP. XVIII]   LITANY TO THOTH.   99

100   THE BOOK OF THE DEAD.   [Chap. XVIII

LITANY TO THOTH. 101

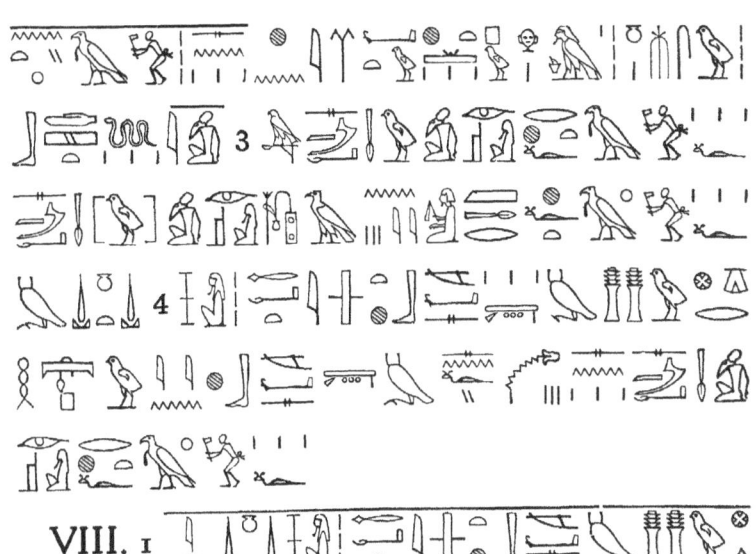

VIII. 1

102　　　　THE BOOK OF THE DEAD.　　[Chap. XVIII

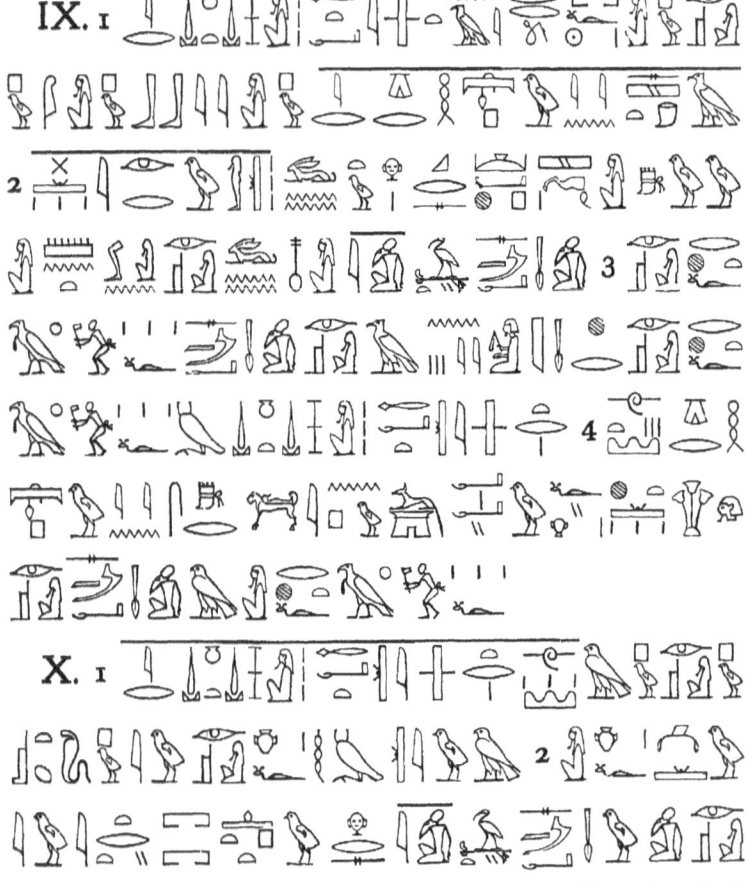

LITANY TO THOTH. 103

RUBRIC.

6

B

104 THE BOOK OF THE DEAD. [Chap. xix

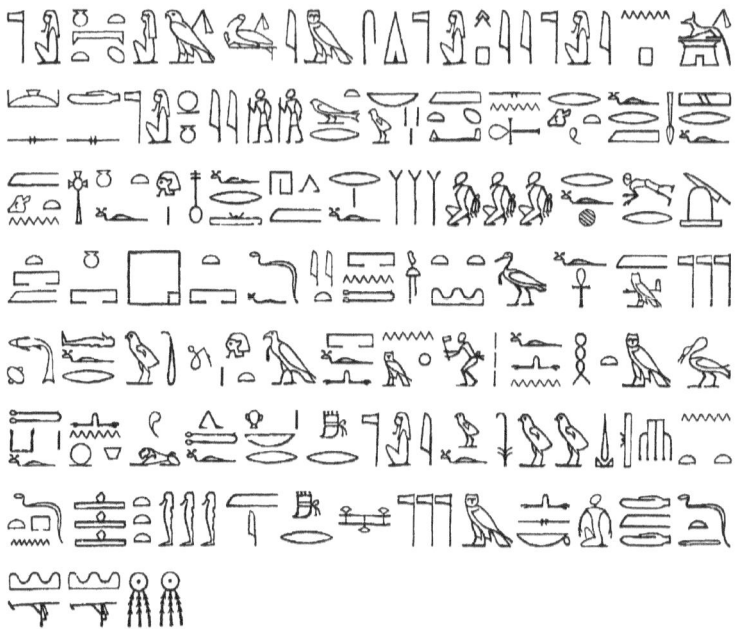

Chapter XIX.

[A. From the Papyrus of Netchemet (Brit. Mus. No. 10,490, plate 7).]
[B. From Lepsius, *Todtenbuch*, Bl. 13.]
[C. From the Coffin of Panehem-Àst (ed. Bergmann, *Jahrbuch*, I, 1, Vienna, 1884).]

THE CROWN OF TRIUMPH.

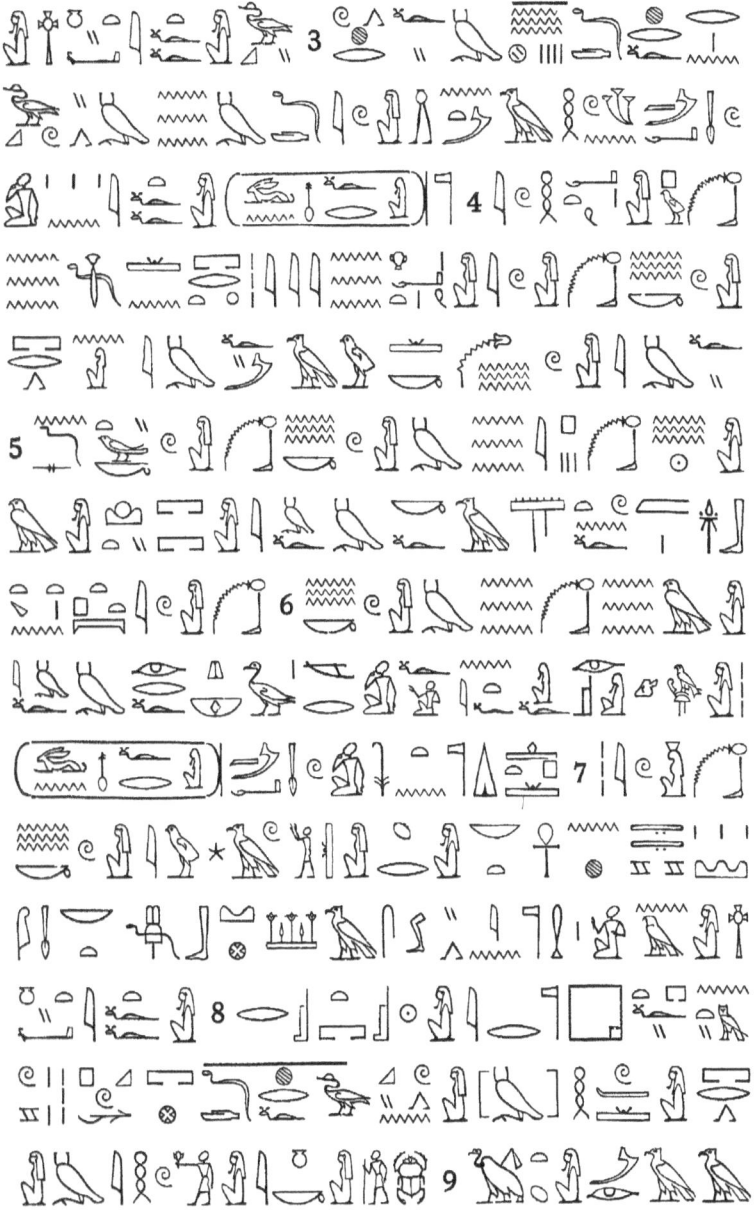

10
11
12
13
14
15

CHAP. XIX] THE CROWN OF TRIUMPH. 107

THE CROWN OF TRIUMPH.

110 THE BOOK OF THE DEAD. [Chap. XIX

THE CROWN OF TRIUMPH. 111

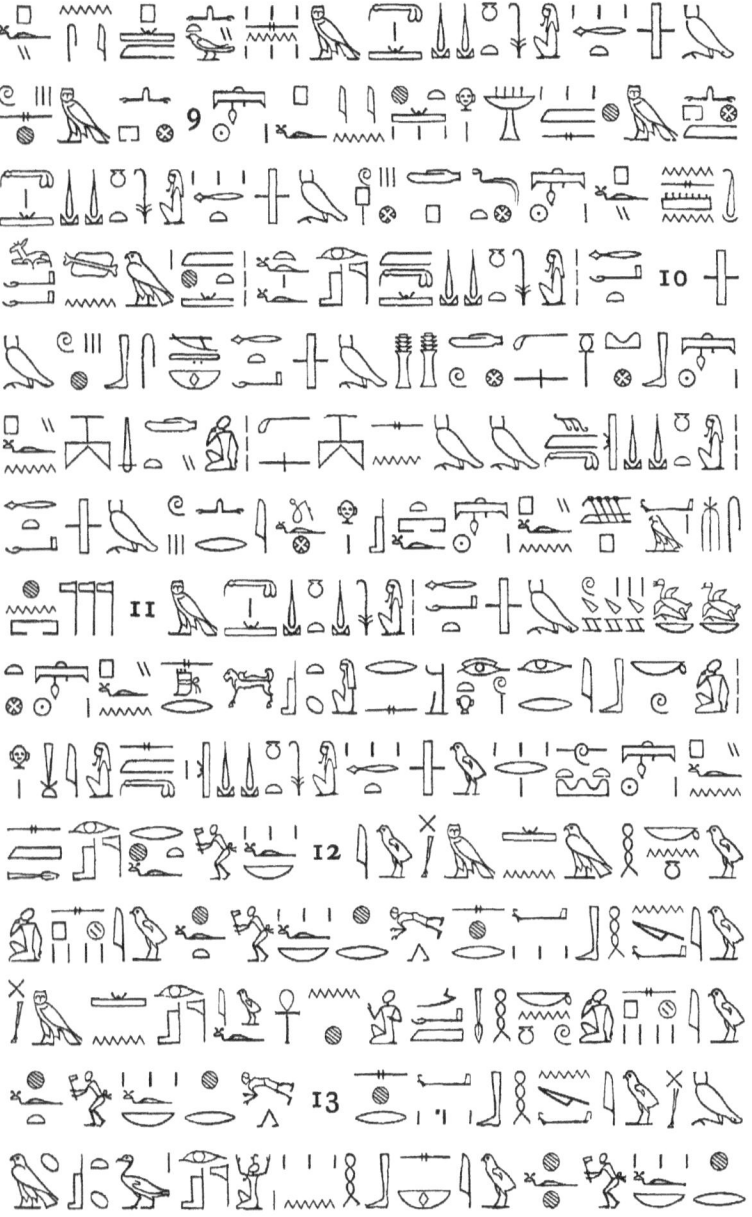

112 THE BOOK OF THE DEAD. [Chap. xix

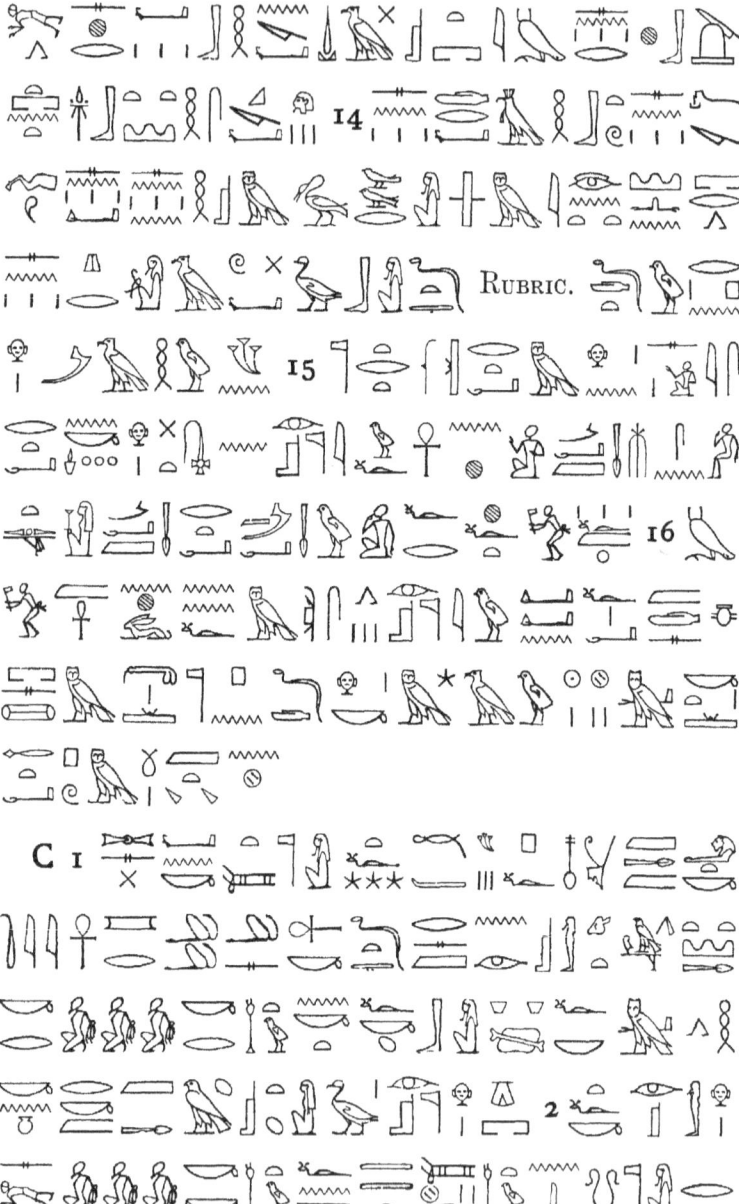

THE CROWN OF TRIUMPH.

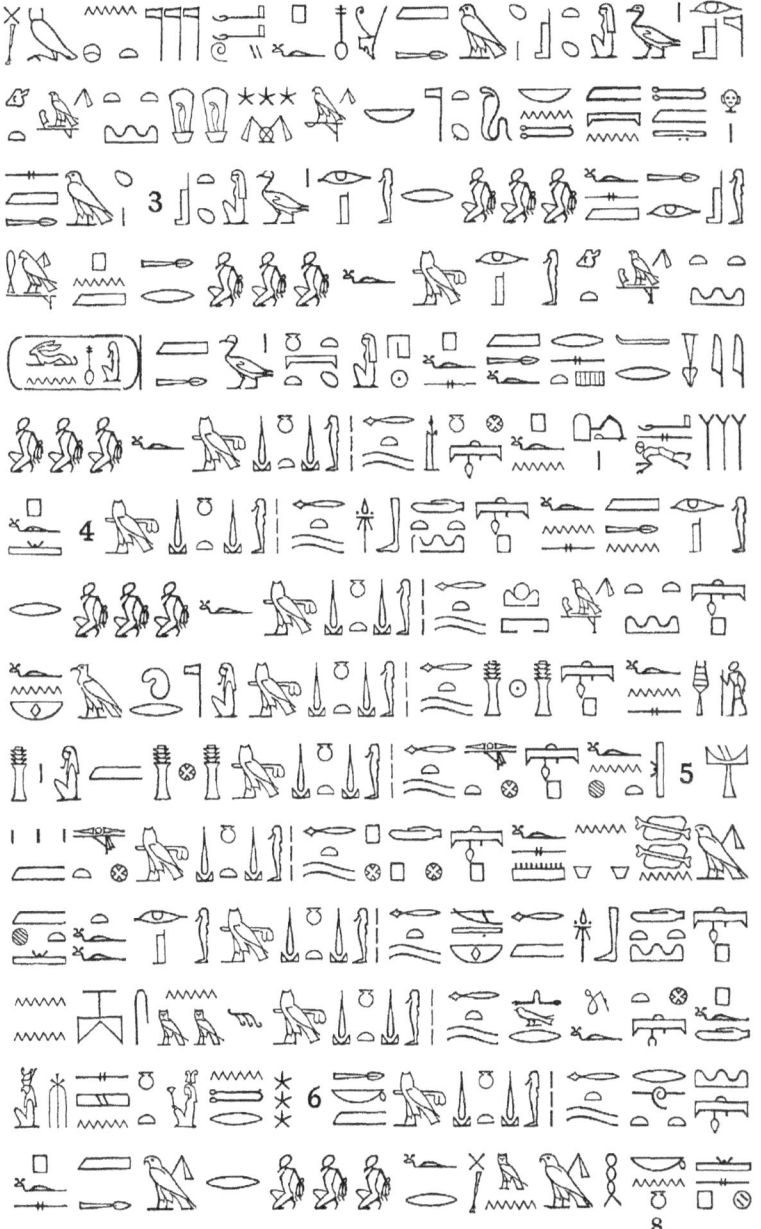

114 THE BOOK OF THE DEAD. [Chap. xix

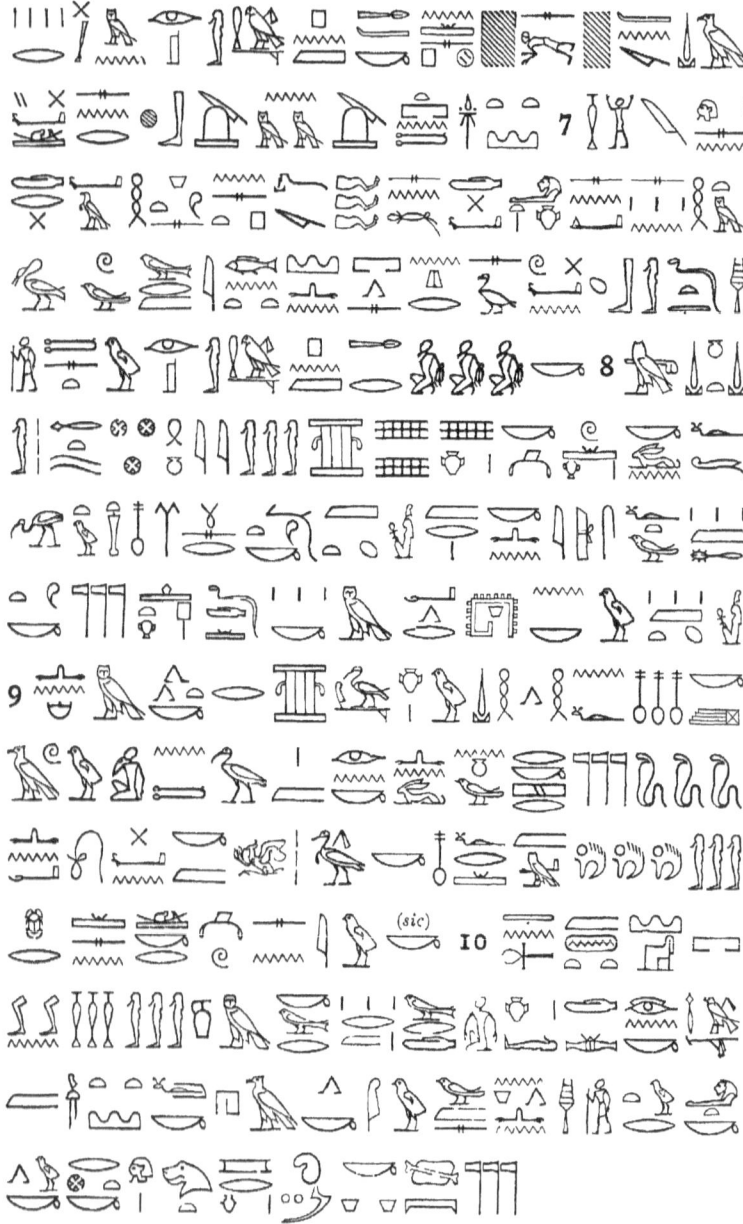

CHAP. XX] LITANY TO THOTH. 115

CHAPTER XX.

[A. From the Papyrus of Nebseni (Brit. Mus. No. 9,900, sheets 11, 12).]
[B. From Lepsius, *Todtenbuch*, Bl. 14]

8*

116 THE BOOK OF THE DEAD. [CHAP. XX

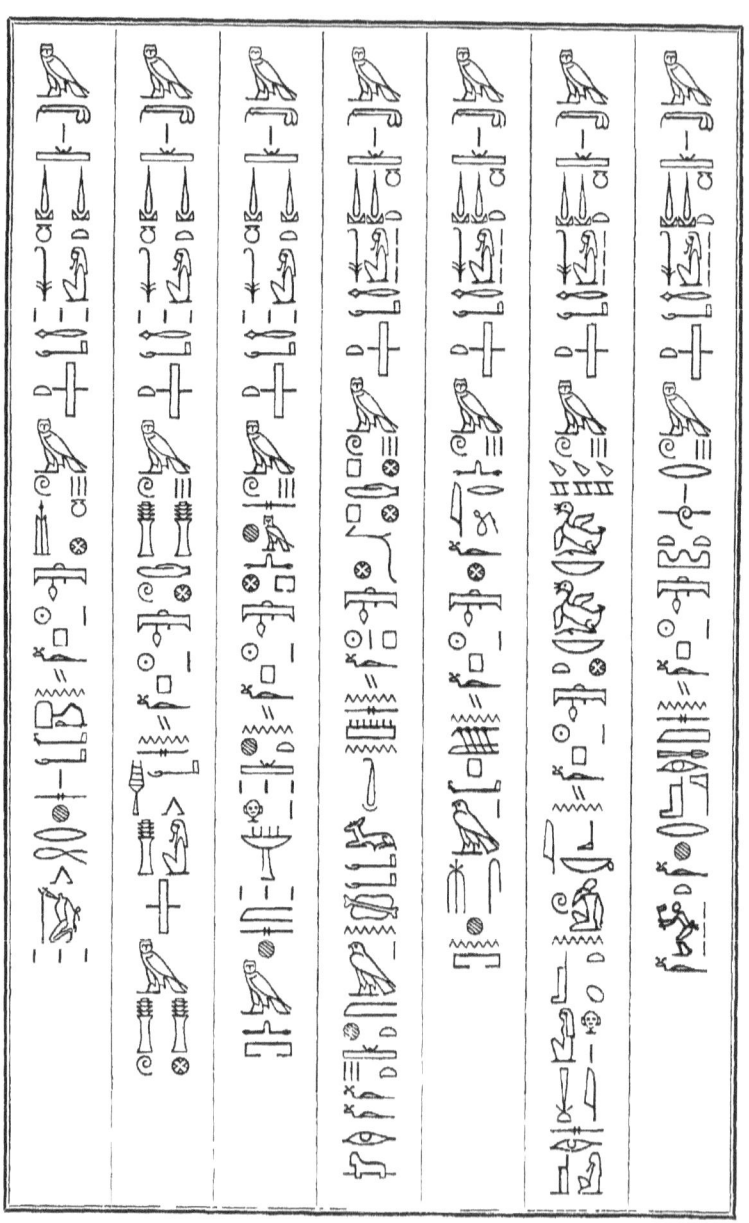

LITANY TO THOTH (Saïte Recension).

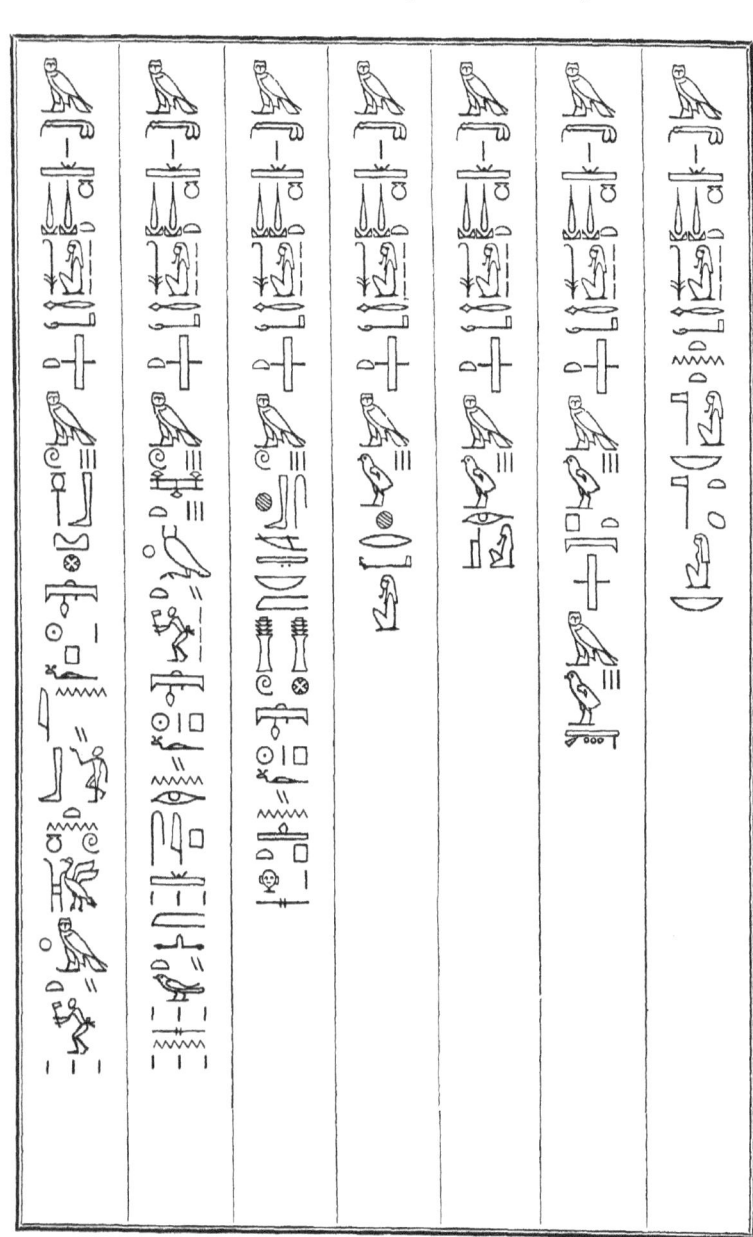

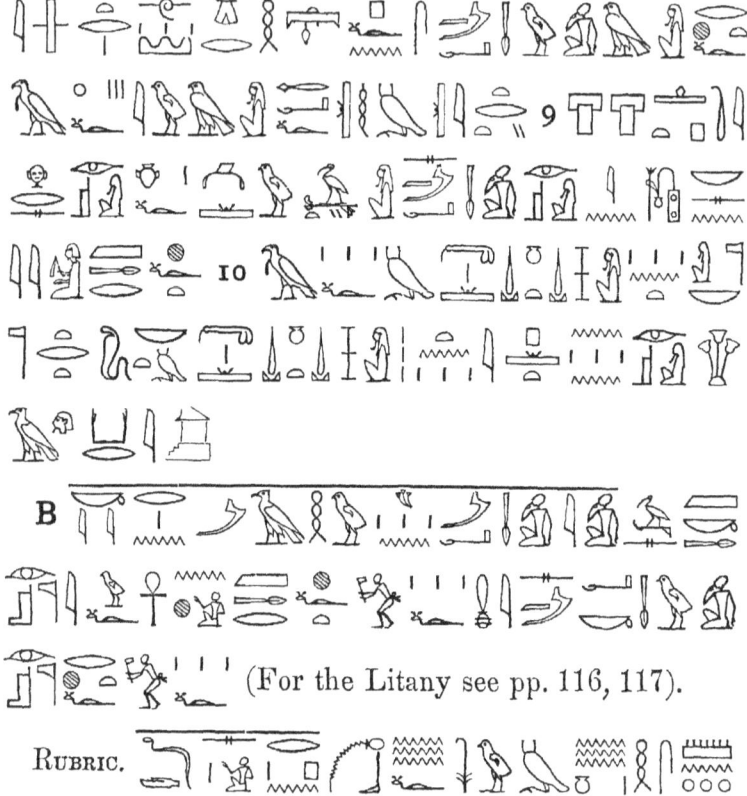

(For the Litany see pp. 116, 117).

Rubric.

Chapter XXI.
[From the Papyrus of Nu (Brit. Mus. No. 10,477, sheet 9).]

Chap. XXII] OF GIVING A HEART. 119

Chapter XXII.

[From the Papyrus of Ani (Brit. Mus. No. 10,470, sheet 6).]

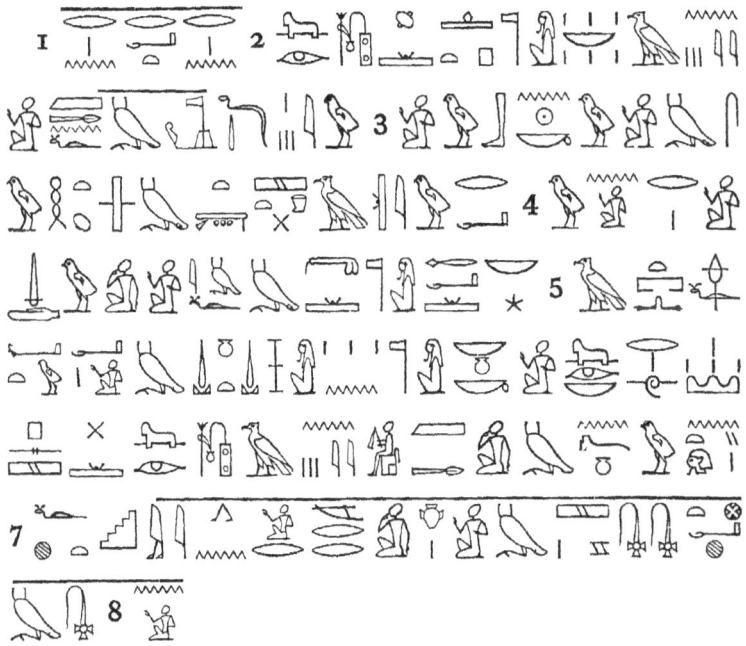

Chapter XXIII.

[From the Papyrus of Ani (Brit. Mus. No. 10,470, sheet 15).]

Chapter XXIV.

[From the Papyrus of Ani (Brit. Mus. No. 10,470, sheet 15).]

CHAP. XXV] OF GIVING MEMORY. 121

CHAPTER XXV.

[From the Papyrus of Nu (Brit. Mus. No. 10,477, sheet 5).]

122 THE BOOK OF THE DEAD. [Chap. XXVI

Chapter XXVI.

[From the Papyrus of Ani (Brit. Mus. No. 10,470, sheet 15).]

OF GUARDING THE HEART.

CHAPTER XXVII.

[From the Papyrus of Ani (Brit. Mus. No. 10,470, sheets 15 and 16).]

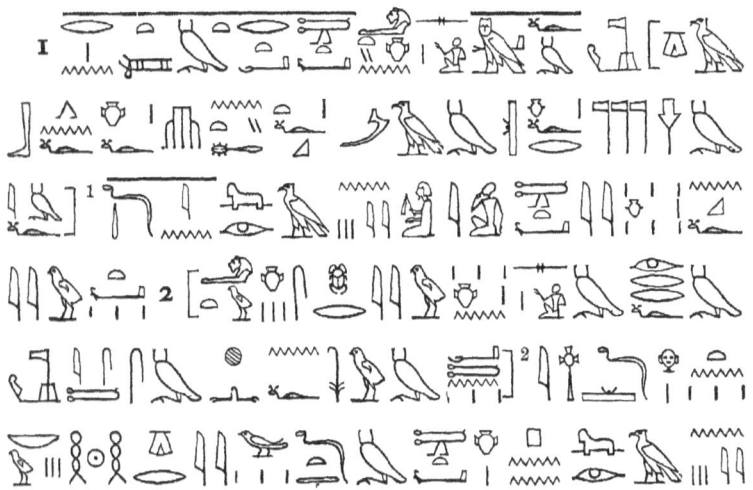

1. From the Papyrus of Mesemneter.
2. From the Papyrus of Nu (sheet 5).

Chapter XXVIII.

[From the Papyrus of Nu (Brit. Mus. No. 10,477, sheet 5).]

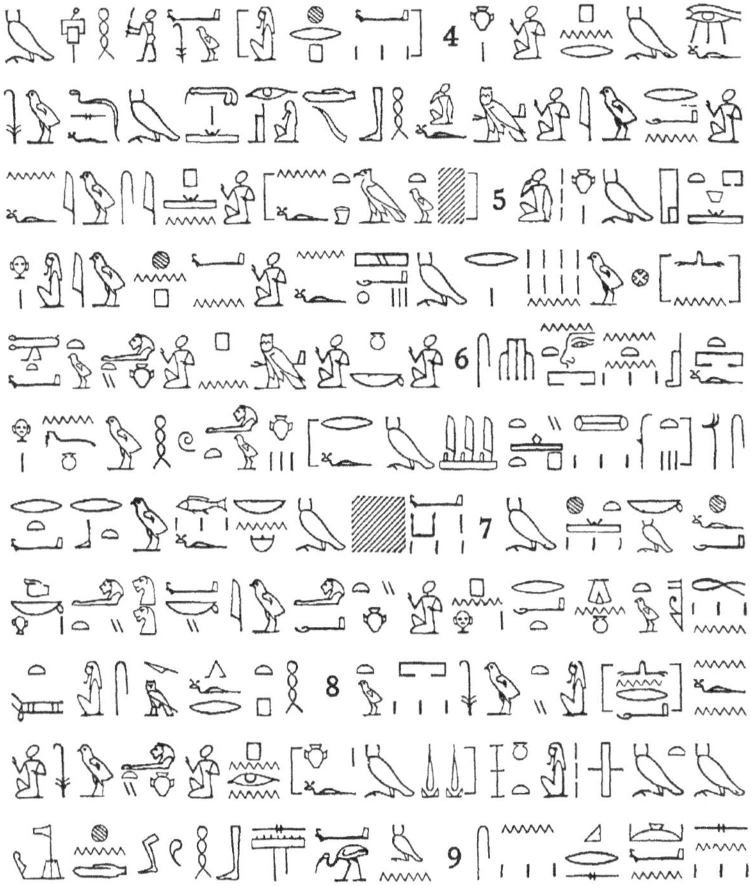

CHAP. XXIX] OF GUARDING THE HEART. 125

CHAPTER XXIX.

[A. From the Papyrus of Ani (Brit. Mus. No. 10,470, sheet 15).]
[B. From the Papyrus of Nu (Brit. Mus. No. 10,477, sheet 12).]

126 THE BOOK OF THE DEAD. [Chap. XXIX A

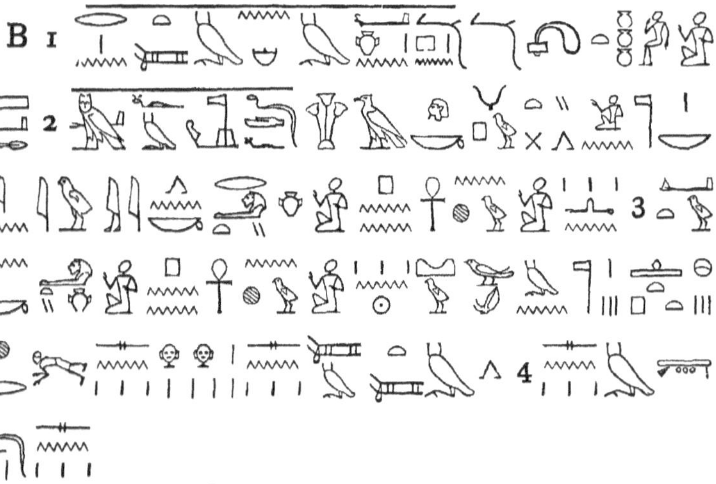

Chapter XXIX A.

[From the Papyrus of Āmen-ḥetep (Naville, *Todtenbuch*, Bd. 1, Bl. 40).]

Chapter XXIX B.

[From the Papyrus of Ani (Brit. Mus. No. 10,477, sheet 33)]

Chapter XXX.

[From Lepsius, *Todtenbuch*, Bl. 16.]

Chapter XXX A.

[From the Papyrus of Nu (Brit. Mus. No. 10,477, sheet 5).]

CHAP. XXX B] OF GUARDING THE HEART. 129

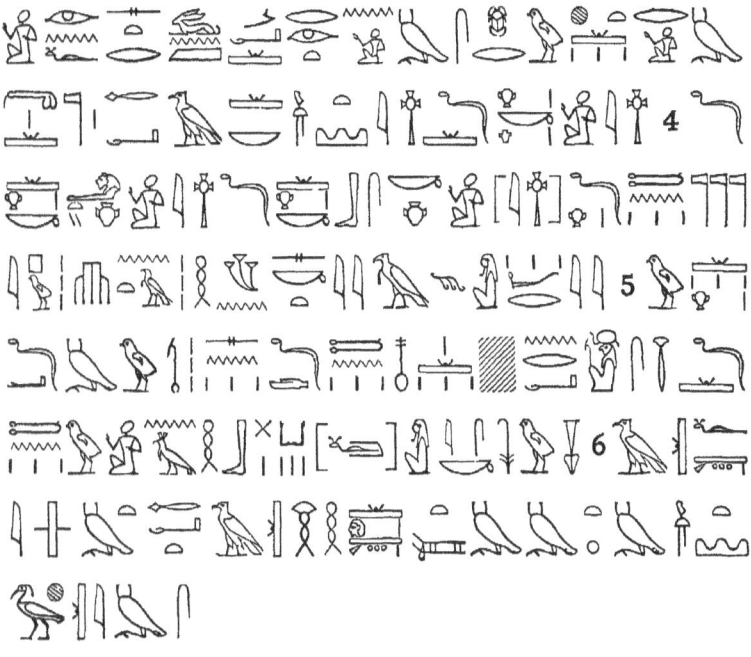

CHAPTER XXX B.

[The title is from the Papyrus of Ani (Brit. Mus. No. 10,470, sheet 15).]
[A. From the Papyrus of Nu (Brit. Mus. No. 10,477, sheet 21).]
[B. From the Papyrus of Iuâu (ed. Naville, plate XVI).]

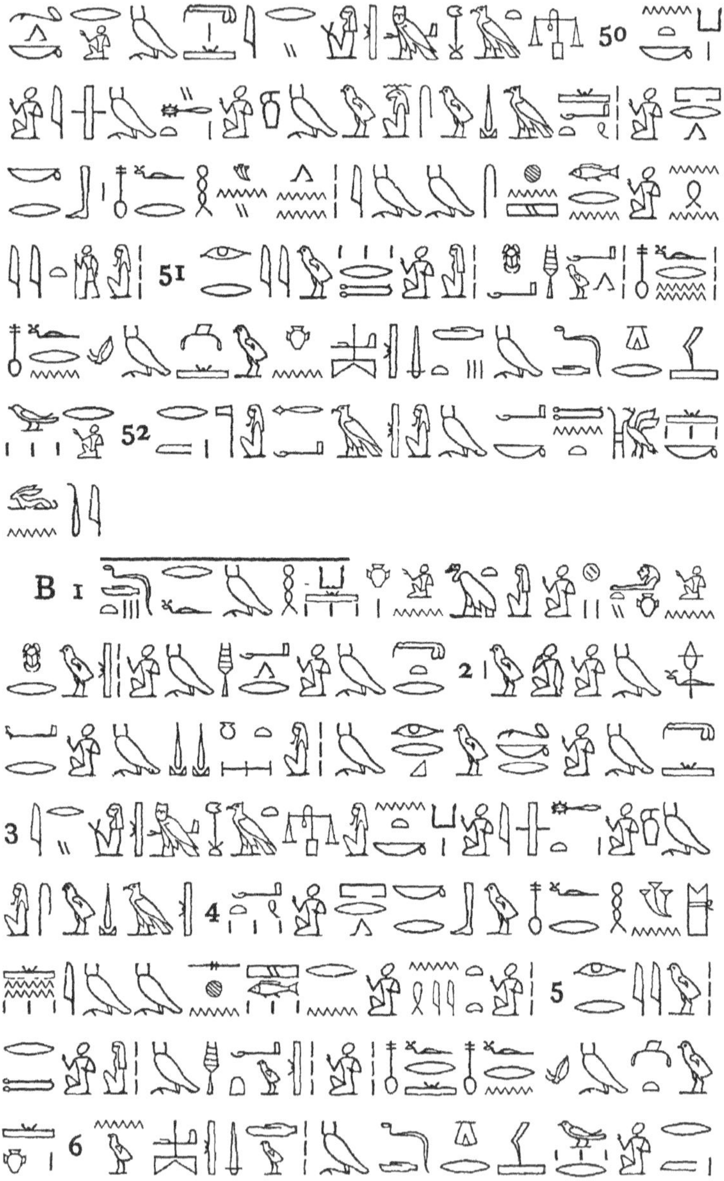

CHAP. XXX B] DISCOVERY OF THE CHAPTER. 131

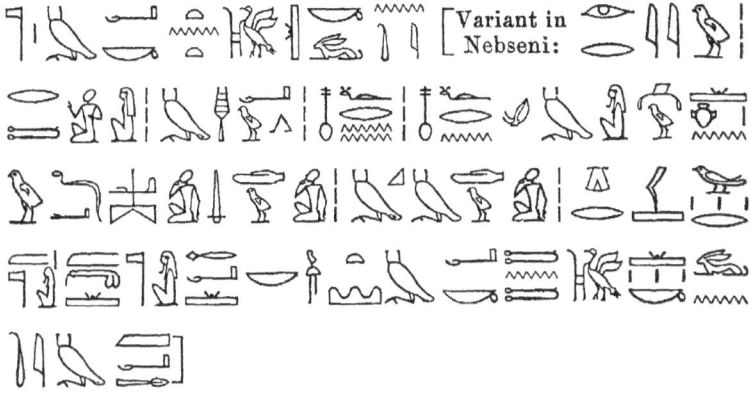

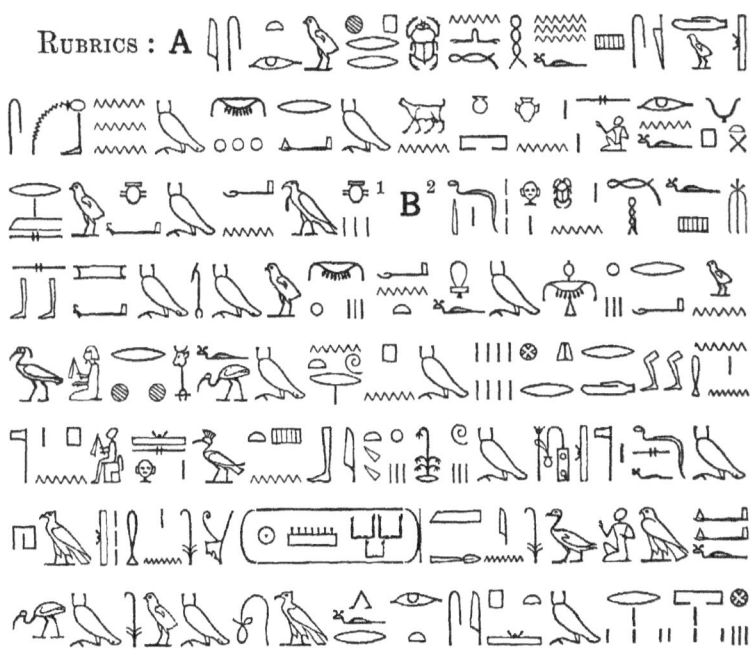

1. From the Papyrus of Nu (sheet 21).
2. From the Papyrus of Âmen-ḥetep (Naville, *Todtenbuch*, Bd. II, p. 99).

Chapter XXXI.

[From the Papyrus of Nu (Brit. Mus. No. 10,477, sheet 5).]

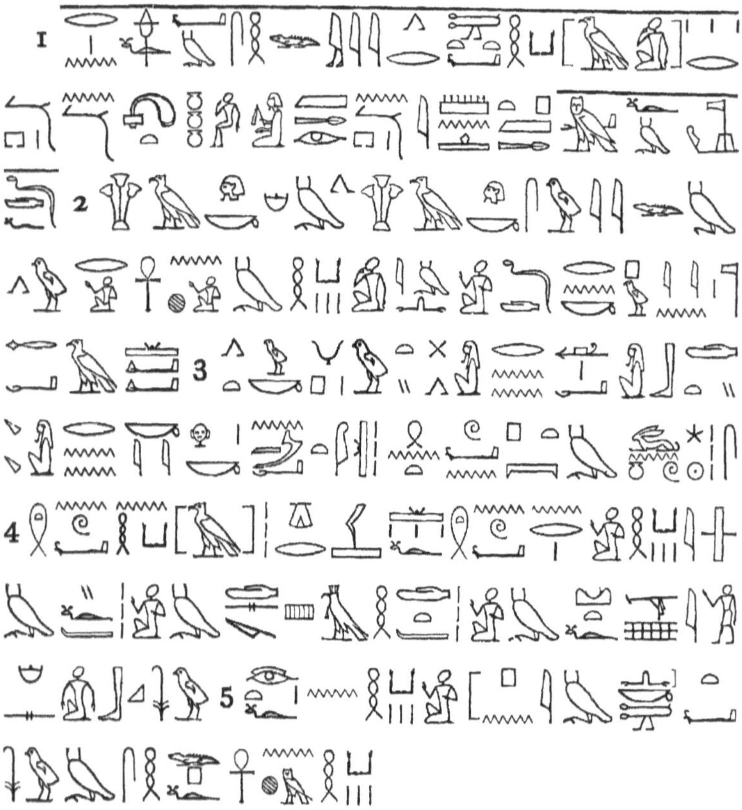

Chapter XXXII.

[From Lepsius, *Todtenbuch*, Bl. 16.]

CHAP. XXXII]   OF REPULSING THE CROCODILE.   133

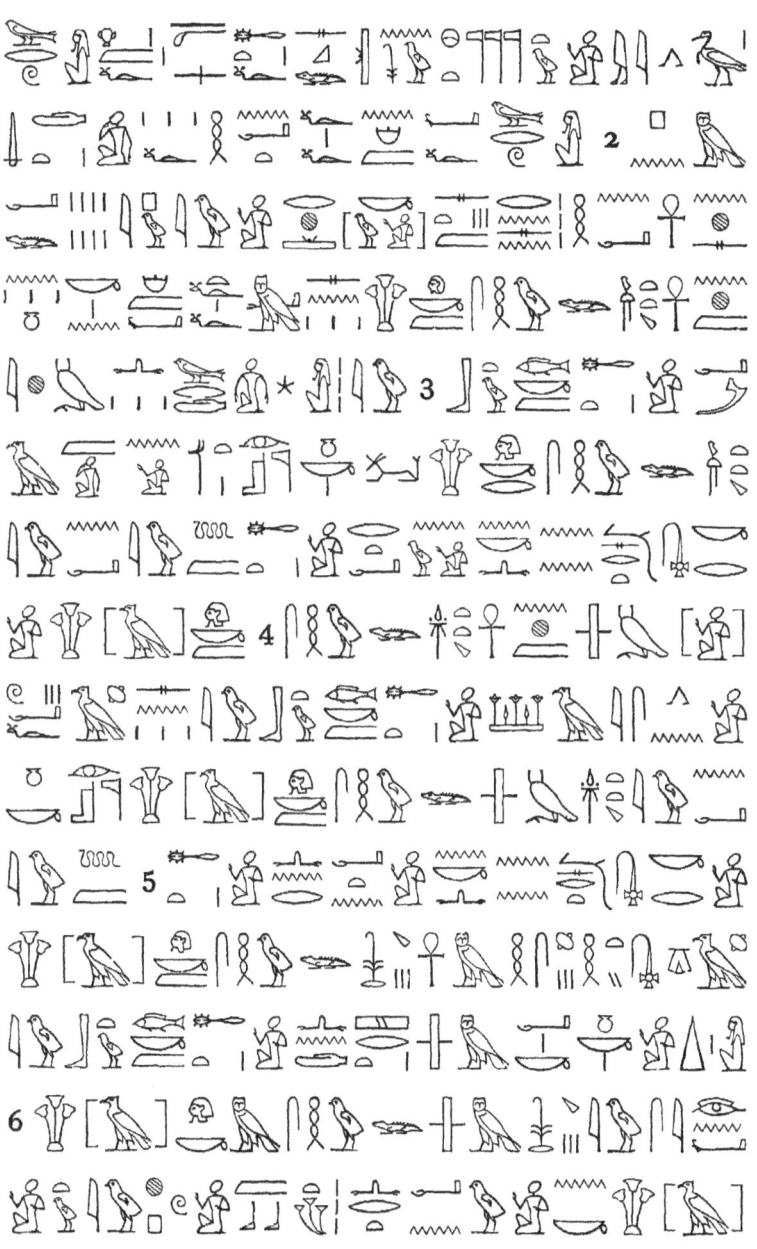

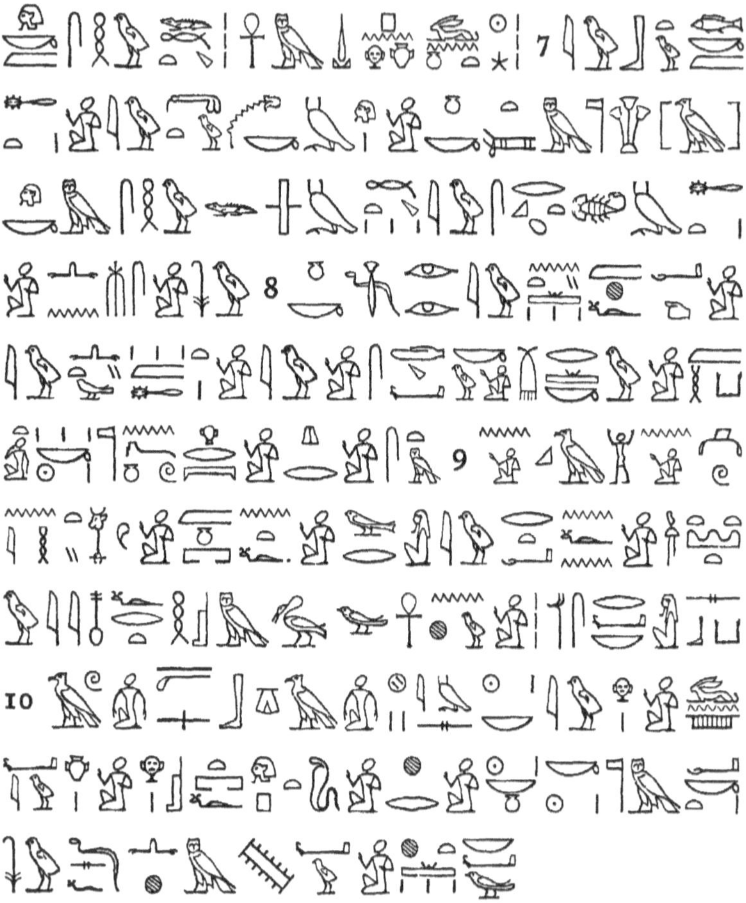

134 THE BOOK OF THE DEAD. [Chap. XXXIII

Chapter XXXIII.

[From the Papyrus of Nu (Brit. Mus. No. 10,477, sheet 6).]

CHAPS. XXXIV, XXXV] OF NOT BEING EATEN. 135

Chapter XXXIV.

[From the Papyrus of Nu (Brit. Mus. No. 10,477, sheet 6).]

Chapter XXXV.

[From the Papyrus of Nu (Brit. Mus. No. 10,477, sheet 6).]

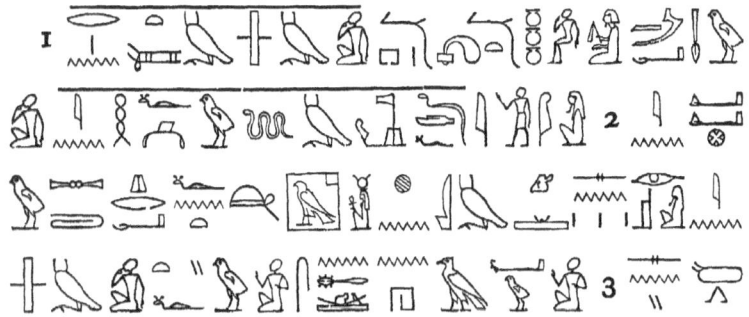

Chapter XXXVI.

[From the Papyrus of Nu (Brit. Mus. No. 10,477, sheet 8).]

Chapter XXXVII.

[From the Papyrus of Nu (Brit. Mus. No. 10,477, sheet 8).]

Chapter XXXVIII A.

[From the Papyrus of Nebseni (Brit. Mus. No. 9,900, sheet 12).]

138   THE BOOK OF THE DEAD.   [Chap. XXXVIII B

Chapter XXXVIII B.

[From the Papyrus of Nu (Brit. Mus. No. 10,477, sheet 12).]

OF REPULSING REREK. 139

Chapter XXXIX.

[From the Papyrus of Mes-em-neter (Naville, *Todtenbuch*, I, Bl. 53).]

140   THE BOOK OF THE DEAD.   [Chap. xxxix

OF REPULSING REREK.

142 THE BOOK OF THE DEAD. [CHAP. XL

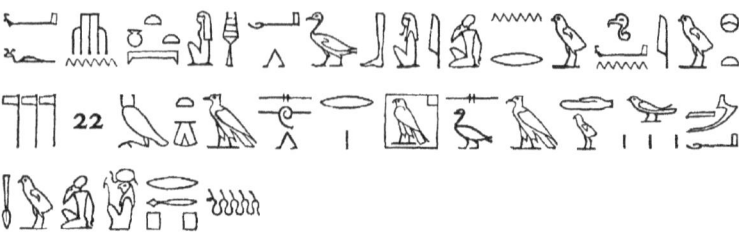

CHAPTER XL.

[A. From the Papyrus of Nu (Brit. Mus. No. 10,477, sheet 8).]
[B. From the Papyrus of Rā (Naville, *Todtenbuch*, Bd. I, Bl. 54).]

CHAP. XL] REPULSING THE EATER OF THE ASS. 143

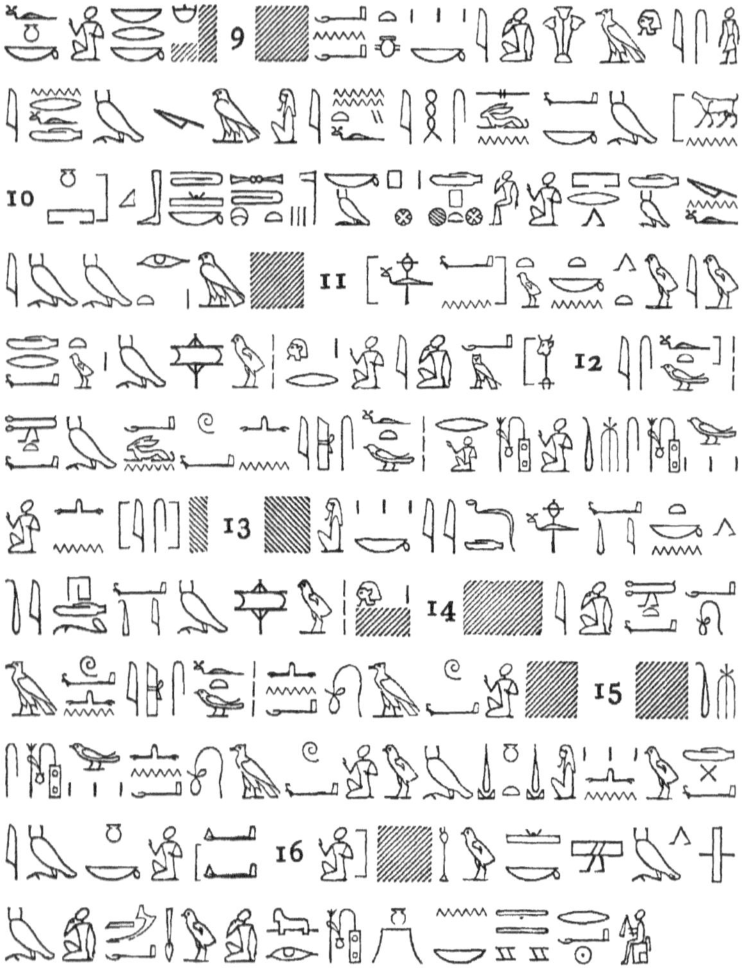

CHAPTER XLI.

[From the Papyrus of Nebseni (Brit. Mus. No. 9,900, sheet 25)]

OF DRIVING AWAY SLAUGHTER.   145

146 THE BOOK OF THE DEAD. [Chap. XLII

Chapter XLII.

[From the Papyrus of Nu (Brit. Mus. No. 10,477, sheet 6).]

CHAP. XLII]   OF DRIVING AWAY SLAUGHTER.   147

1. From the Papyrus of Mesemneter.

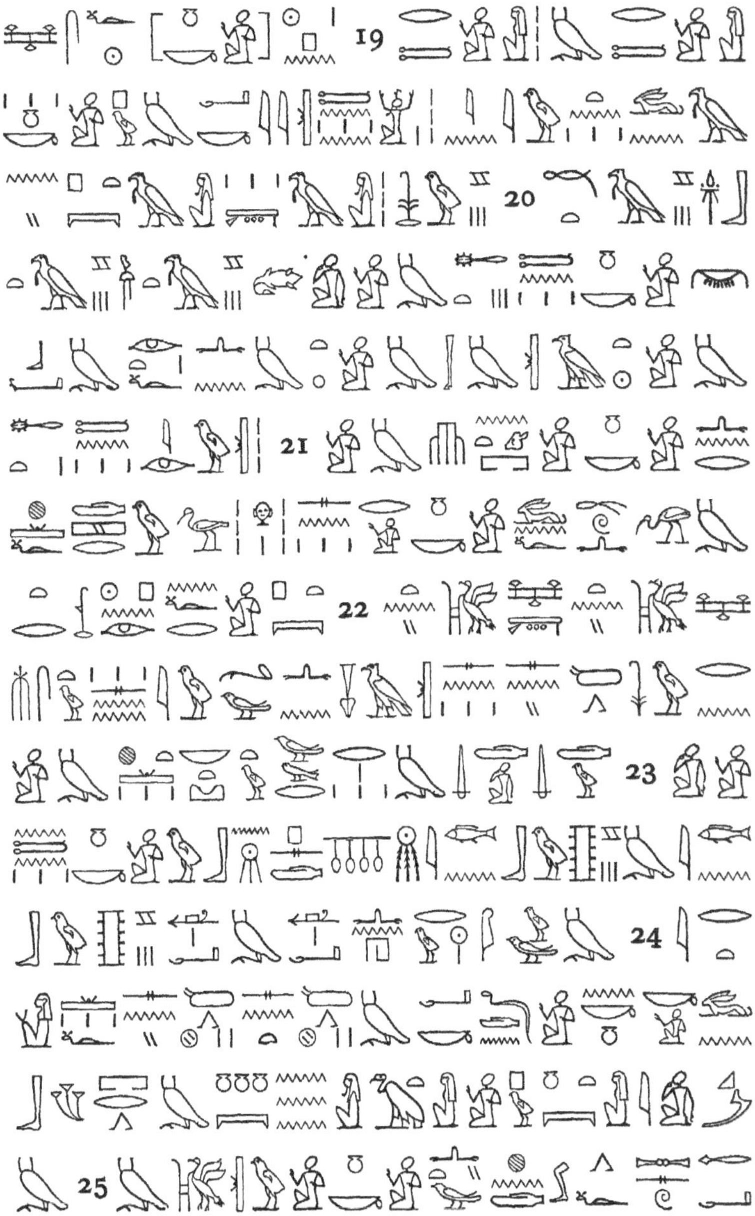

CHAP. XLII]   OF DRIVING AWAY SLAUGHTER.

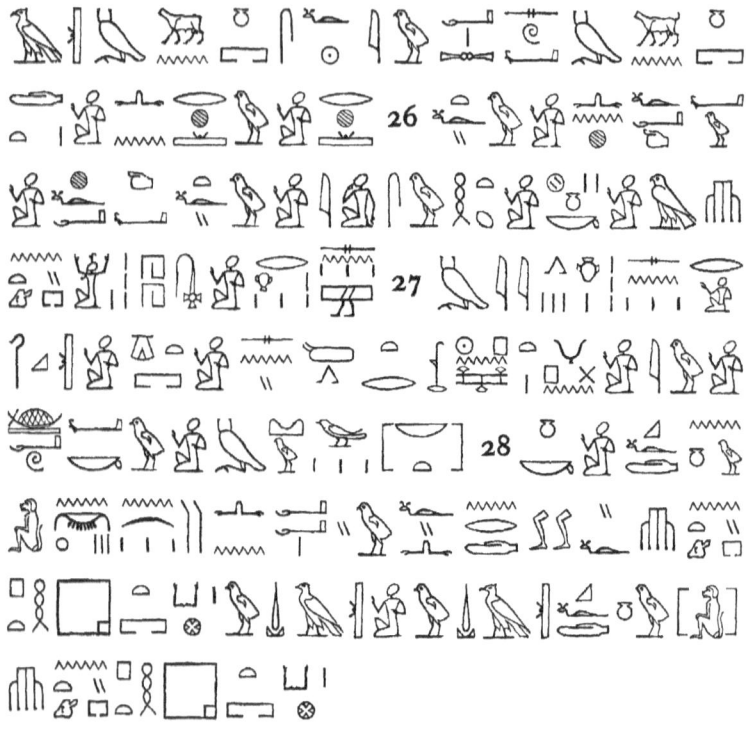

Chapter XLII.

[From the Papyrus of Ani (Brit. Mus. No. 10,470, sheet 32).]

In the Papyrus of Ani only a portion of this Chapter is given, *i. e.,* the section which gives the names of the deities with whom the various members of the body of the deceased are identified; it is arranged in tabular form and is printed on pp. 151, 152, 153.

CHAP. XLII] THE DEIFICATION OF MEMBERS.

152   THE BOOK OF THE DEAD.   [Chap. XLII

CHAP. XLII]   THE DEIFICATION OF MEMBERS.   153

154 THE BOOK OF THE DEAD. [CHAP. XLIII

CHAPTER XLIII.

[A. From the Papyrus of Nu (Brit. Mus. No. 10,477, sheet 5).]
[B. From the Papyrus of Ani (Brit. Mus. No. 10,470, sheet 17).]

CHAPS. XLIV, XLV] OF AVOIDING THE SECOND DEATH. 155

CHAPTER XLIV.

[From the Papyrus of Ani (Brit. Mus. No. 10,470, sheet 16).]

CHAPTER XLV.

[From the Papyrus of Ani (Brit. Mus. No. 10,470, sheet 16).]

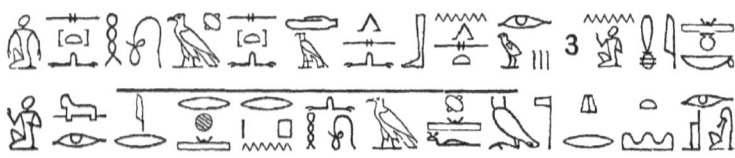

Chapter XLVI.

[A. From the Papyrus of Nebseni (Brit. Mus. No. 9,900, sheet 5).]
[B. From the Papyrus of Nu (Brit. Mus. No. 10,477, sheet 12).]
[C. From the Papyrus of Ani (Brit. Mus. No. 10,470, sheet 16).]

Chapter XLVII.

[From the Papyrus of Nu (Brit. Mus. No. 10,477, sheet 8).]

Chapter XLVIII.
(See Chapter X.)

Chapter XLIX.
(See Chapter XI.)

Chapter L A.

[From the Papyrus of Nebseni (Brit. Mus. No. 9,900, sheet 12).]

158   THE BOOK OF THE DEAD.   [Chap. L B

Chapter L B.

[From the Papyrus of Nu (Brit. Mus. No. 10,477, sheet 19).]

CHAPTER LI.

[From the Papyrus of Nu (Brit. Mus. No. 10,477, sheet 8).]

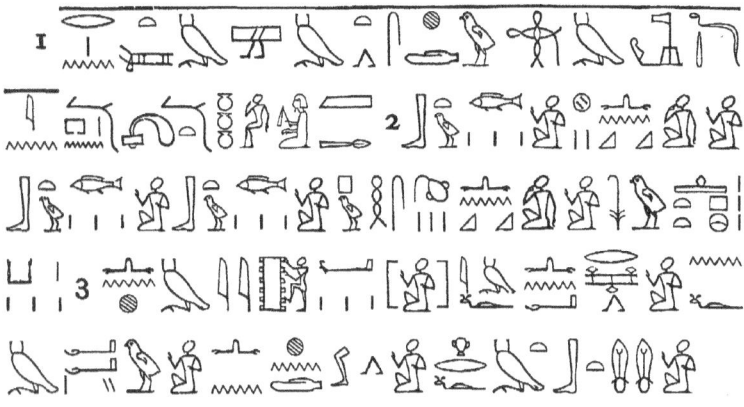

CHAPTER LII A.

[From the Papyrus of Nu (Brit. Mus. No. 10,477, sheet 11).]

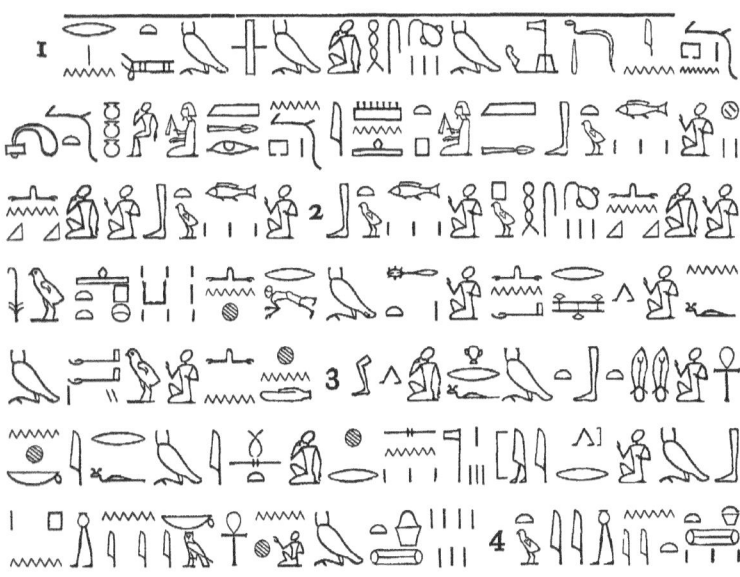

160 THE BOOK OF THE DEAD. [Chap. LII B

Chapter LII B.[1]

[From the Papyrus of Nu (Brit. Mus. No. 10,477, sheet 19).]

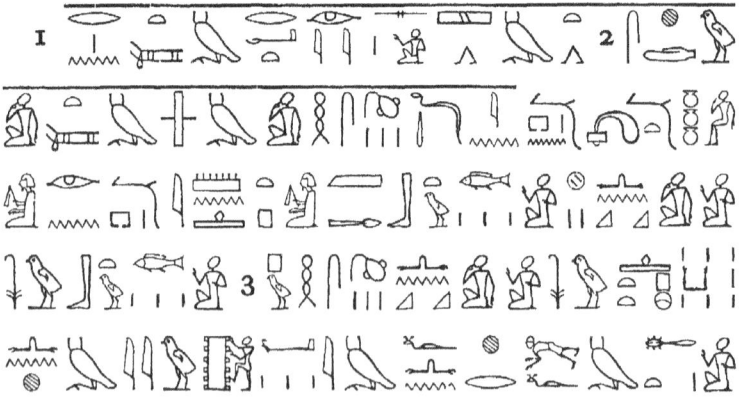

1. I formerly gave this Chapter the number CLXXXIX.

CHAP. LII B] OF NOT EATING FILTH. 161

THE BOOK OF THE DEAD. [Chap. LII B

OF NOT EATING FILTH.

164   THE BOOK OF THE DEAD.   [Chap. LIII

Chapter LIII.

[From the Papyrus of Nu (Brit. Mus. No. 10,477, sheet 11).]

CHAP. LIII] OF AVOIDING FILTH AND FOUL WATER. 165

1. From the Papyrus of Rā (Naville, op. cit., II, 124).

Chapter LIV.

[From the Papyrus of Nu (Brit. Mus. No. 10,477, sheet 12).]

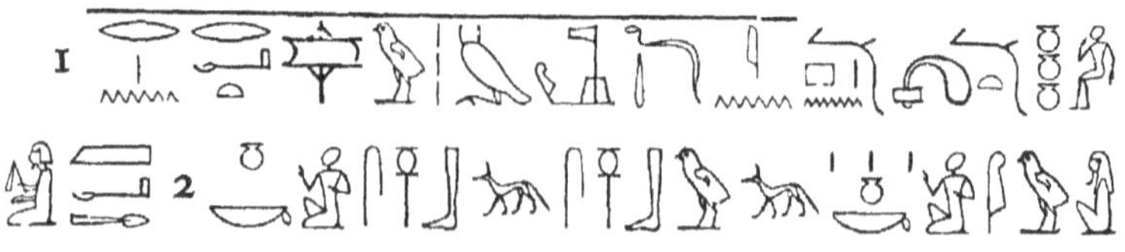

Chapter LV.

[From the Papyrus of Nu (Brit. Mus. No. 10,177, sheet 12).]

OF GIVING AIR IN THE OTHER WORLD.

CHAPTER LVI.

[From the Papyrus of Nu (Brit. Mus. No. 10,477, sheet 12).]

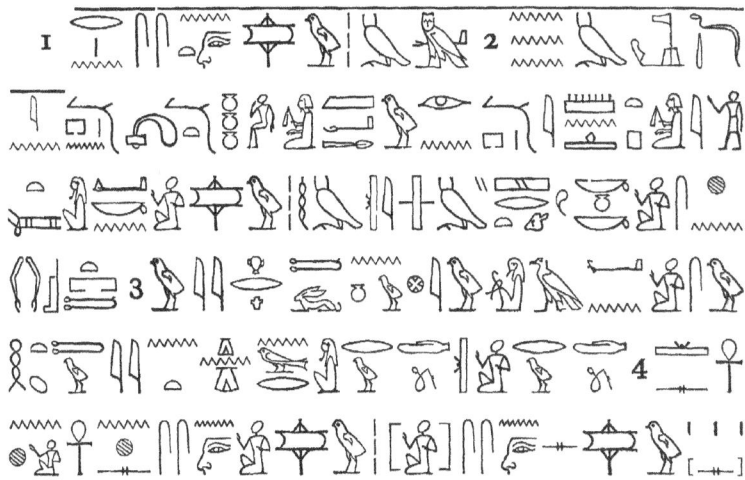

CHAPTER LVII.

[From the Papyrus of Nu (Brit. Mus. No. 10,477, sheet 12).]

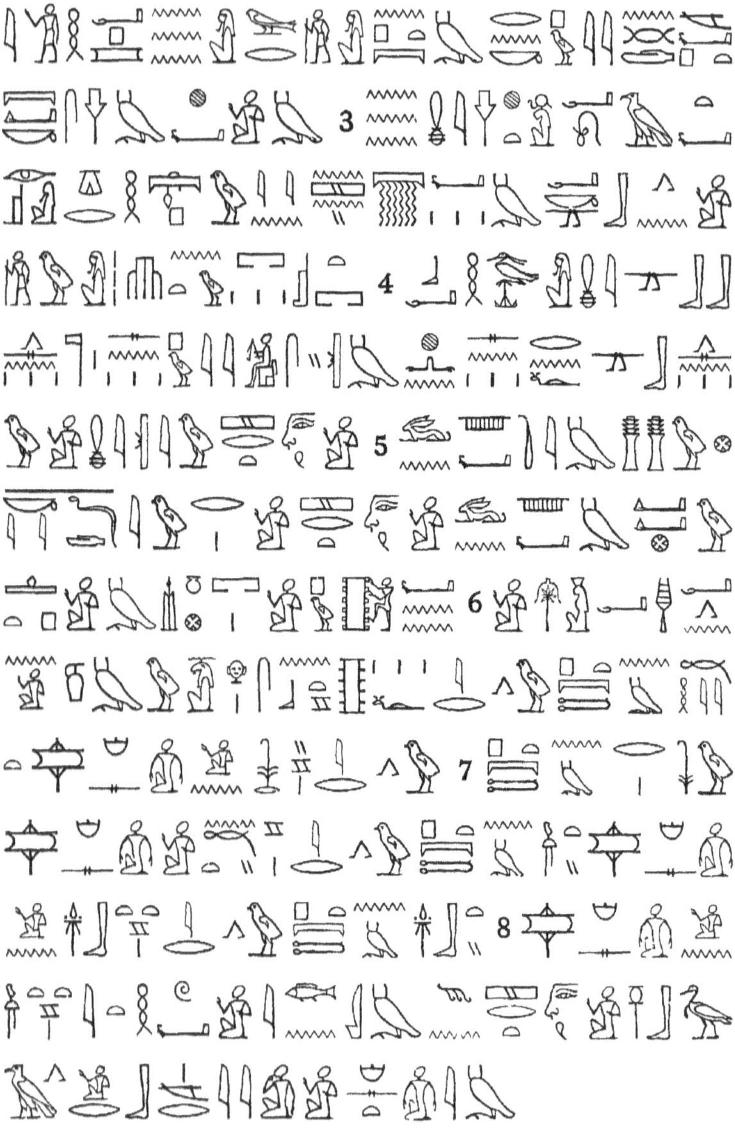

CHAP. LVIII] OF OBTAINING AIR AND WATER. 169

The Chapter ends differently in the Papyrus of Nefer-uben-f, and instead of the section beginning has the following:

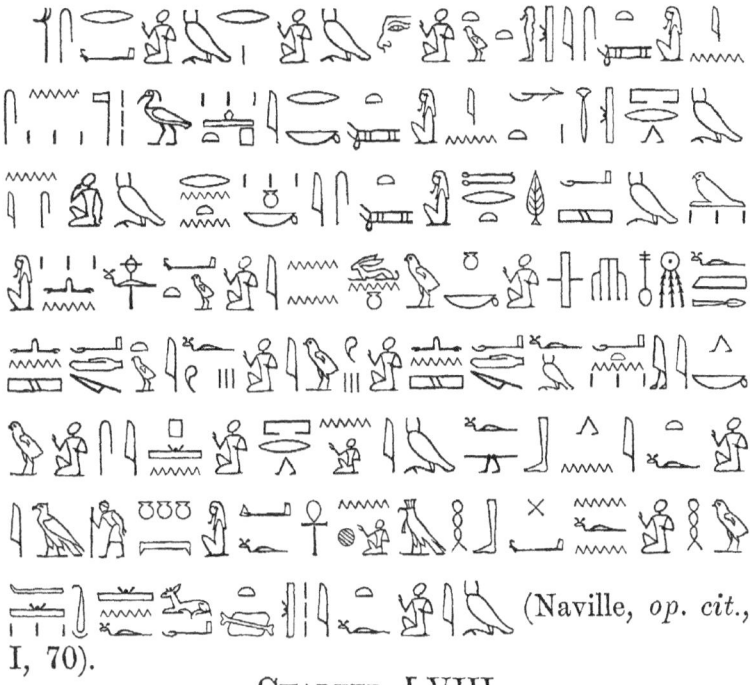

(Naville, op. cit., I, 70).

CHAPTER LVIII.
[From the Papyrus of Ani (Brit. Mus. No. 10,470, sheet 16)]

170   THE BOOK OF THE DEAD.   [Chap. LIX

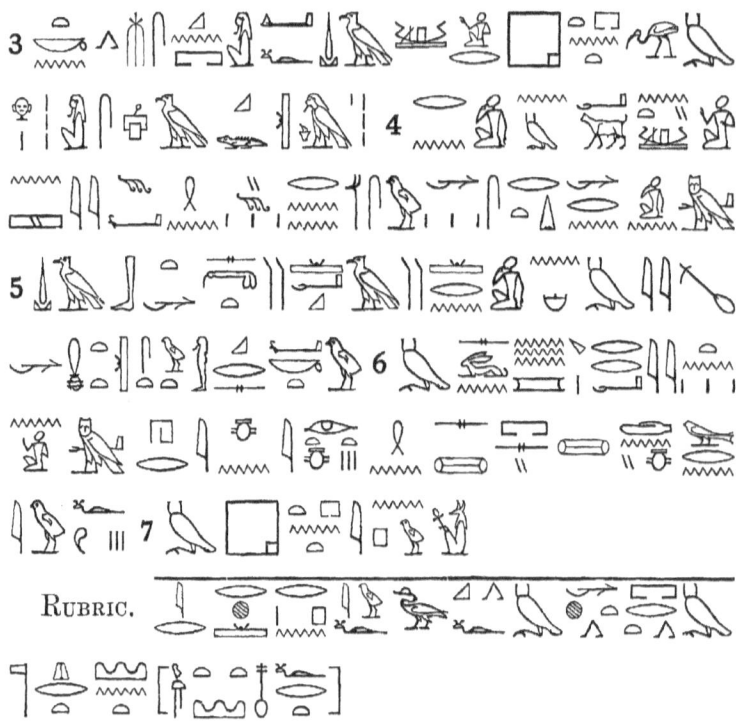

Rubric.

Chapter LIX.

[From the Papyrus of Ani (Brit. Mus. No. 10,470, sheet 16).]

CHAPS. LX, LXI]   OF GUARDING THE SOUL.   171

CHAPTER LX.

[From Lepsius, *Todtenbuch*, Bl. 23.]

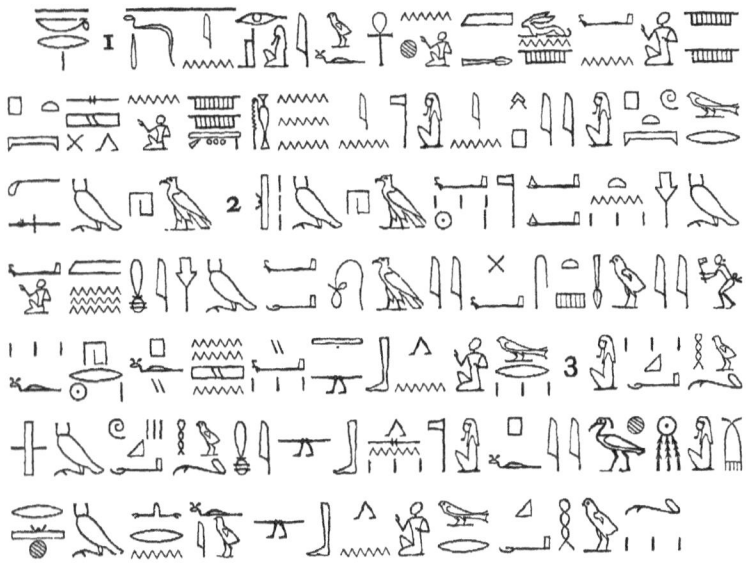

CHAPTER LXI.

[From the Papyrus of Ani (Brit. Mus. No. 10,470, sheet 15).]

172   THE BOOK OF THE DEAD.   [CHAP. LXII

CHAPTER LXII.

[A. From the Papyrus of Nebseni (Brit. Mus. No. 9,900, sheet 4).]
[B. From the Papyrus of Nefer-uben-f (Naville, *op. cit.*, I, 72).]

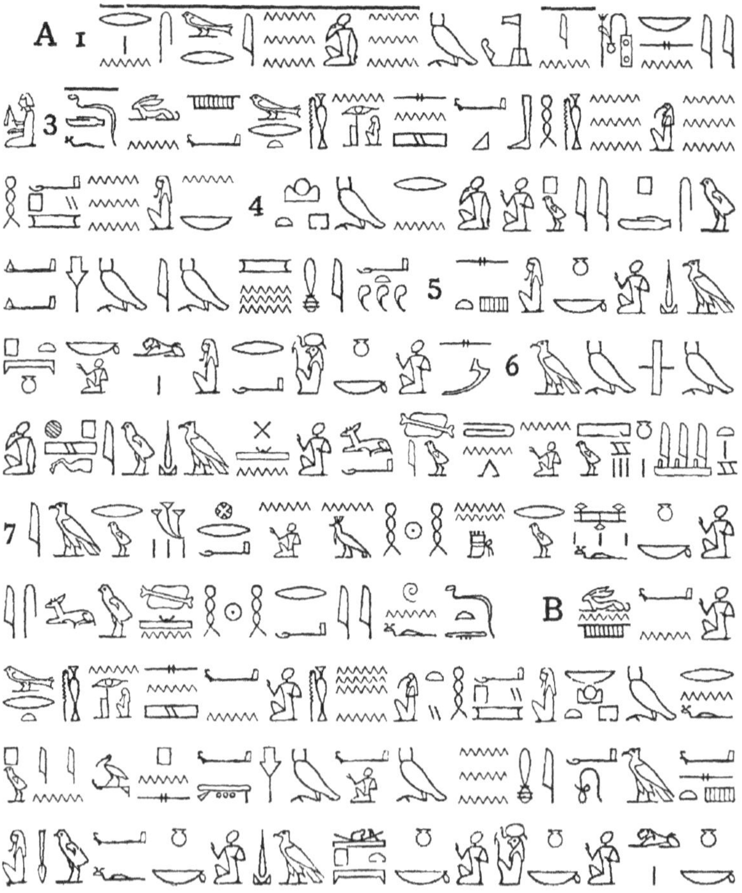

OF AVOIDING SCALDINGS. 173

CHAPTER LXIII A.

[A. From the Papyrus of Nu (Brit. Mus. No. 10,477, sheet 7).]
[B. From the Papyrus of Iuâu (Davis Papyrus, ed. Naville, pl. IX).]

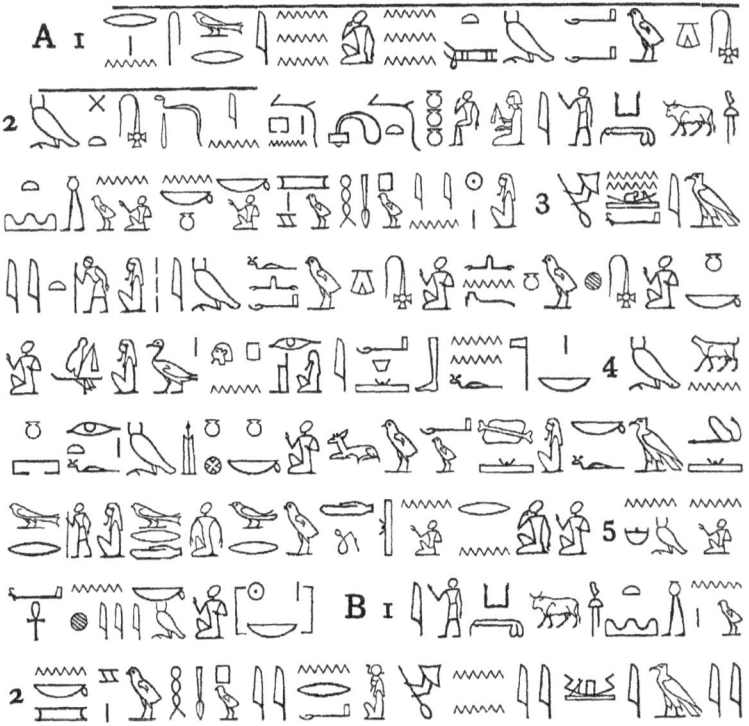

Chapter LXIII B.

[From the Papyrus of Nu (Brit. Mus. No. 10,477, sheet 12).]

Chapter LXIV.

The LXIVth Chapter is one of the oldest and one of the most important Chapters of the Book of the Dead. It exists in two forms, one of which is much longer than the other; both forms are given in the oldest and best manuscripts of the Theban Recension, e. g., the Papyrus of Nu and the Papyrus of Iuàu. The longer form is entitled "The Chapter of Coming Forth by Day in Neter-khert" (i. e., the Other World), and according to the Rubric the text was "found" by Ḥeruṭāṭāf, a son of Cheops, cut on a block of bàa stone (?), in letters of real lapis-lazuli, in the city of Hermopolis in the reign of MEN-KAU-RĀ, the MYKERINOS of the Greeks, a king of the IVth dynasty. It was to be recited by a man who was fasting from meat and fish, and was ceremonially pure, in connection with the Heart Chapter (XXX B), and with the performance of the ceremony of "Opening the Mouth". The shorter form is entitled "The Chapter of knowing "the Chapters of Coming forth by Day in a single "Chapter", and was "found" in the temple of Ḥennu by a chief mason in the reign of SEMTI, a king of the 1st dynasty. Another tradition assigned the composition of the Chapter to the reign of Menthu-ḥetep, presumably one of the kings of the XIth dynasty. The shorter form was probably regarded as an abridgment of all the Chapters of Coming Forth by Day, and it seems to have had a value which was equivalent to them all.

Chapter LXIV. (Long Version.)

[A. From the Papyrus of Nu (Brit. Mus. No. 10,477, sheets 20, 21)]

Chapter LXIV. (Long Version.)

[From the Papyrus of Nebseni (Brit. Mus. No. 9,900, sheets 24 and 25).]

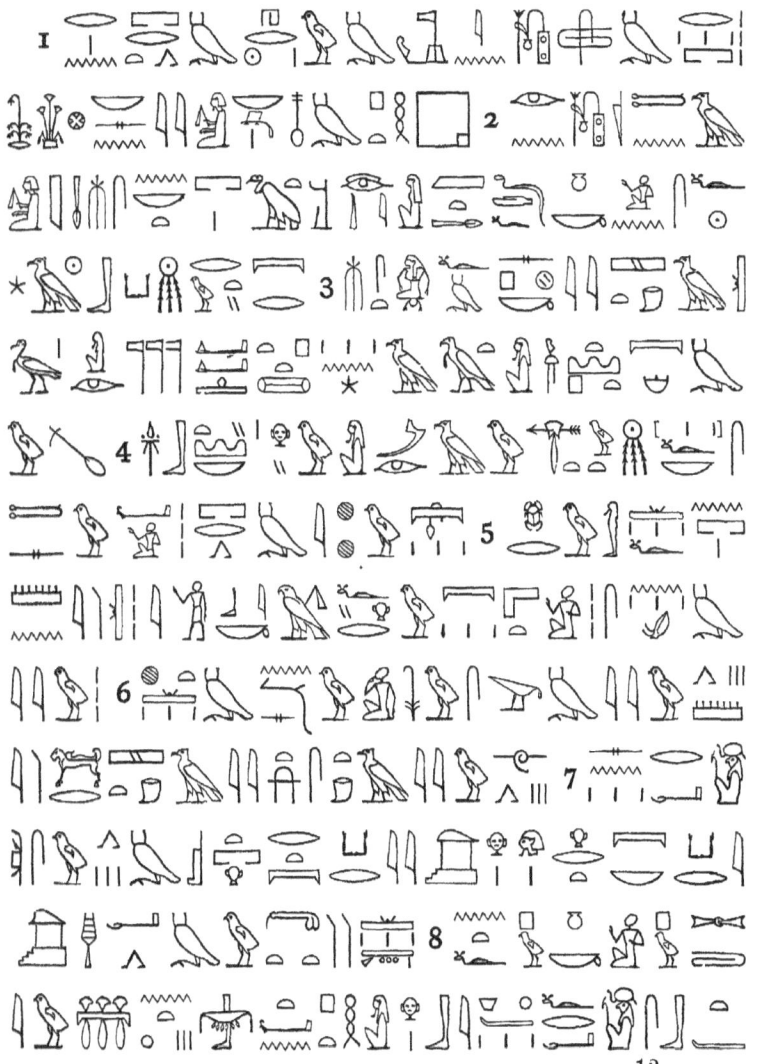

178   THE BOOK OF THE DEAD.   [Chap. LXIV

CHAP. LXIV] OF COMING FORTH BY DAY. 179

180 THE BOOK OF THE DEAD. [Chap. LXIV

CHAP. LXIV] OF COMING FORTH BY DAY. 181

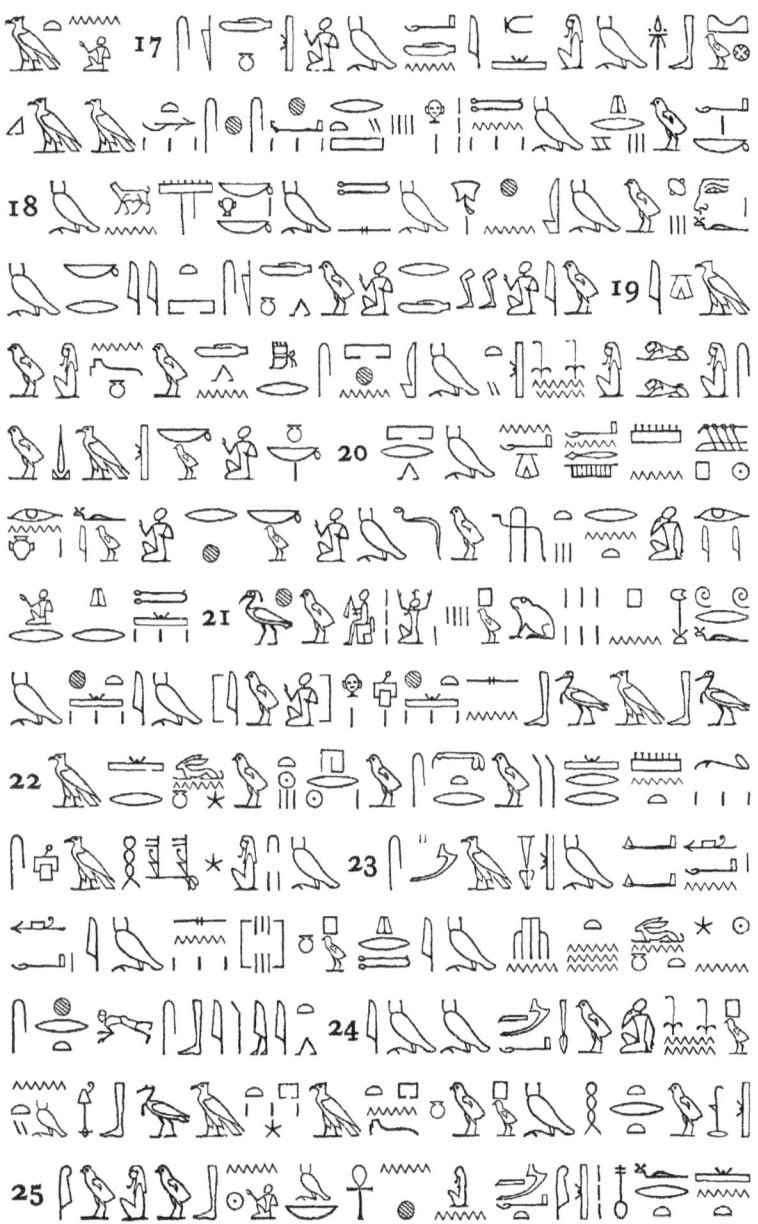

[Chap. LXIV

OF COMING FORTH BY DAY. 183

CHAP. LXIV] OF COMING FORTH BY DAY. 185

186 THE BOOK OF THE DEAD. [Chap. LXIV

Rubric.

CHAP. LXIV]   OF COMING FORTH BY DAY.   187

RUBRIC.

188 THE BOOK OF THE DEAD. [CHAP. LXIV

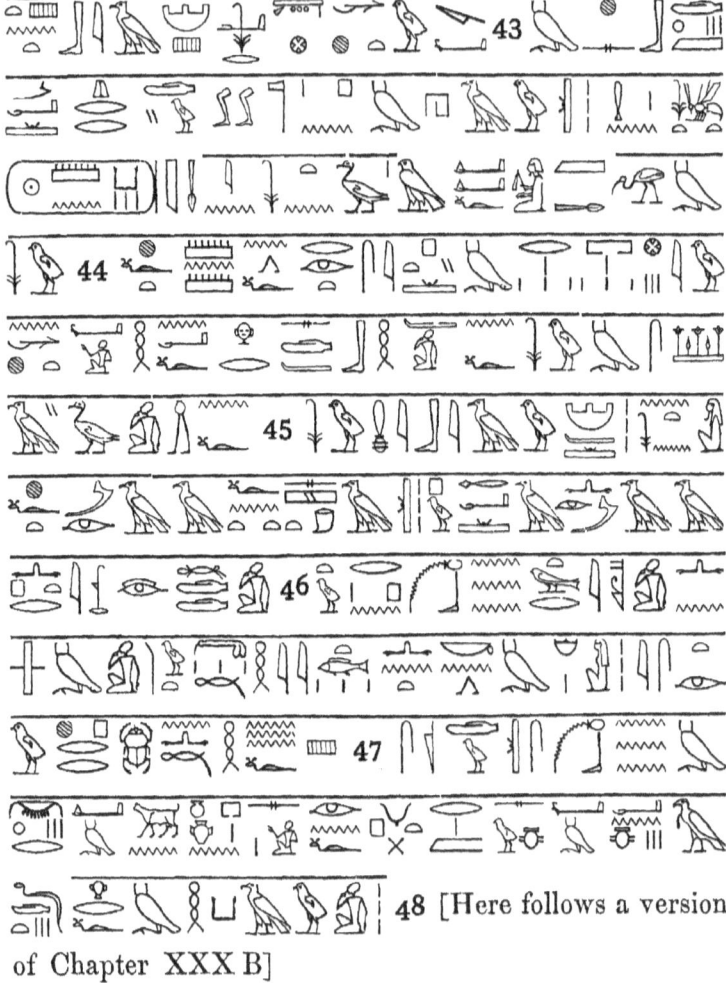

48 [Here follows a version of Chapter XXX B]

OF COMING FORTH BY DAY.

[hieroglyphic text]

Rubric.[1] [hieroglyphic text]

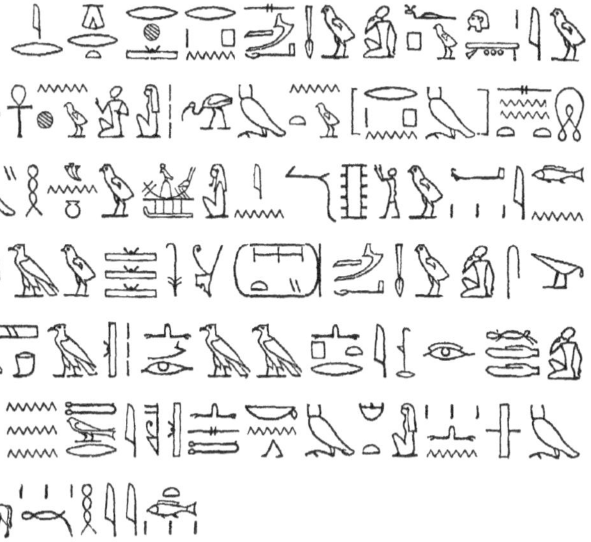

CHAPTER LXIV. (Long Version.)

[From the Papyrus of Iuâu (Davis Papyrus, ed. Naville, plate 15).]

I [hieroglyphic text]

[1] From the Papyrus of Nefer-uben-f (Naville, *op. cit.*, II, p. 139).

OF COMING FORTH BY DAY.

CHAP. LXIV]   DISCOVERY OF ḤERU-ṬĀṬĀF.   193

 etc. (See above, Chapter XXX B)

CHAPTER LXIV. (Short Version.)

[From the Papyrus of Nu (Brit. Mus. No. 10,477, sheet 13).]

[CHAP. LXIV] OF COMING FORTH BY DAY. 195

CHAPTER LXIV. (Short Version.)

[From the Papyrus of Iuȧu (Davis Papyrus, ed. Naville, plate 9).]

13*

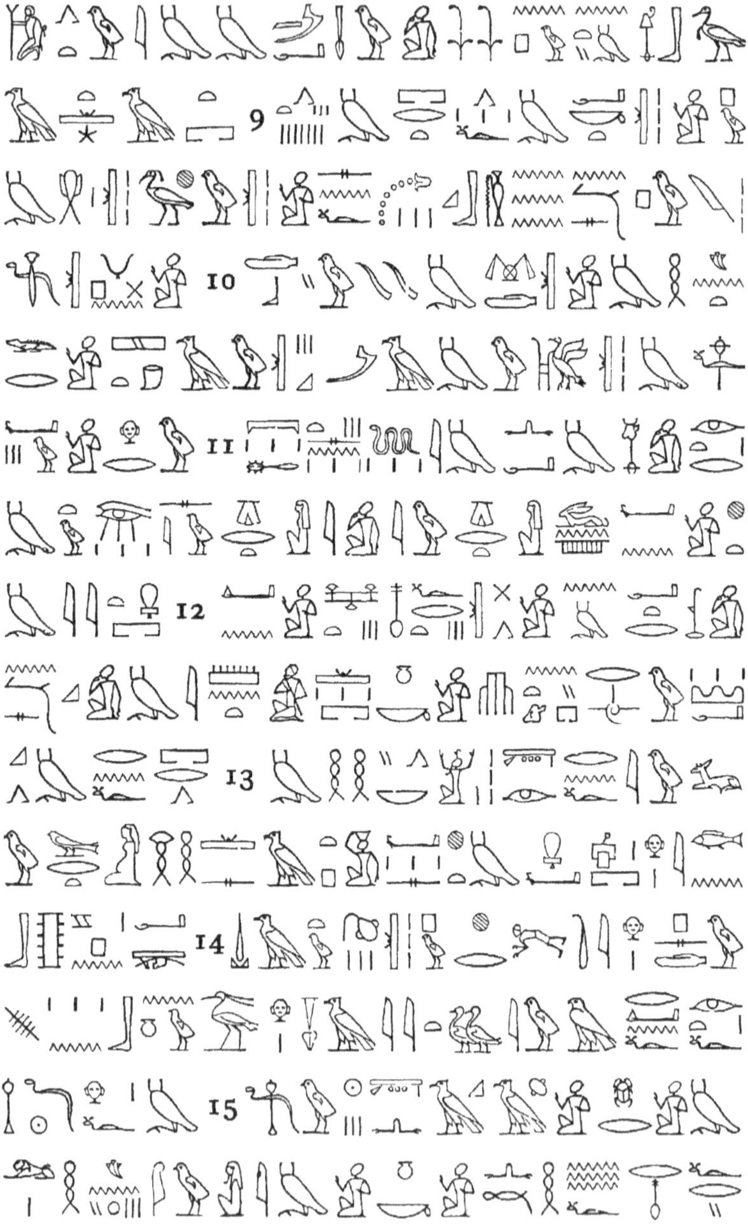

CHAP. LXIV]   OF COMING FORTH BY DAY.   197

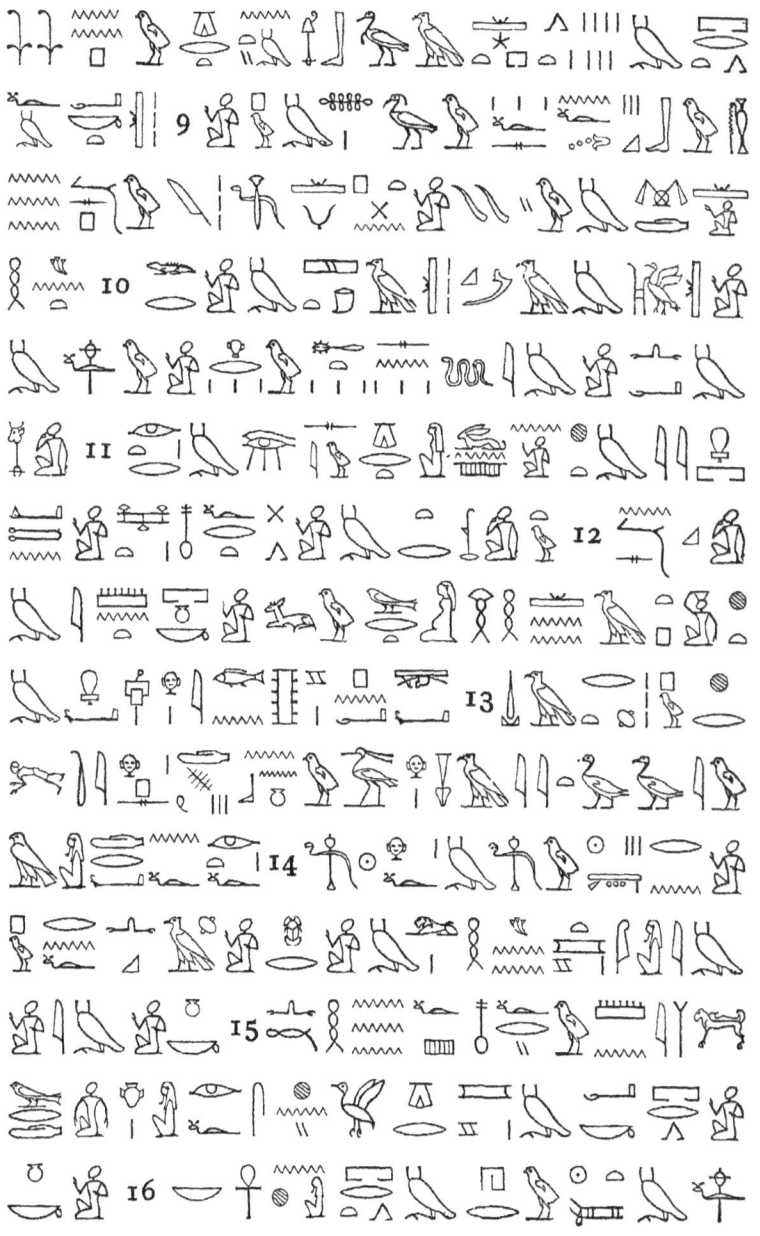

198 THE BOOK OF THE DEAD. [Chap. LXIV

CHAP. LXIV] OF COMING FORTH BY DAY. 199

RUBRIC.

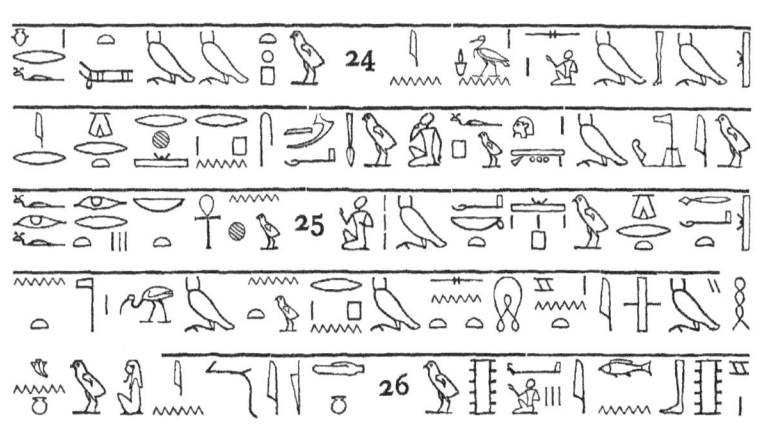

www.ingramcontent.com/pod-product-compliance
Lightning Source LLC
Chambersburg PA
CBHW020327170426
43200CB00006B/295